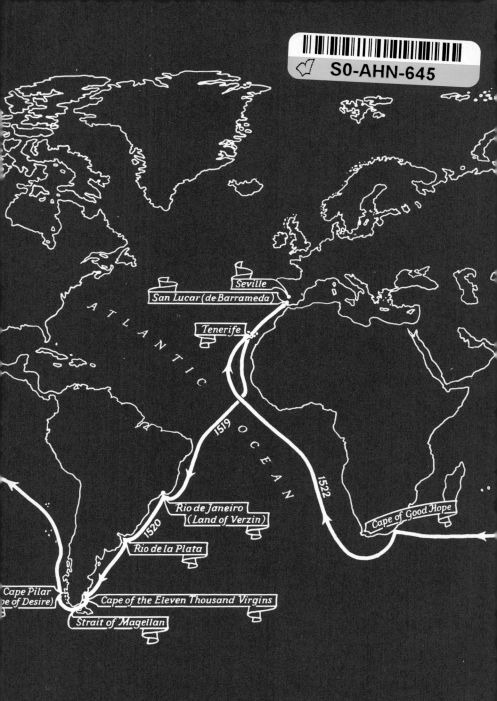

Route of the First Circumnavigation

7/8/75

Ferdinand Magellan

ANTONIO PIGAFETTA

Magellan's Voyage

A Narrative Account of
the First Navigation

Translated and Edited by
R. A. SKELTON
from the manuscript in the Beinecke
Rare Book and Manuscript Library of
Yale University

London: The Folio Society
MCMLXXV

PRINTED IN GREAT BRITAIN

by W & J Mackay Limited, Chatham

Illustrations

Ferdinand Magellan *frontispiece*
   Portrait by unknown artist. Vienna, Kunsthistorisches Museum, photo Mayer, Vienna

FACSIMILE PAGES

from the manuscript in the Beinecke Rare Book and Manuscript Library of Yale University

The publishers would like to thank the owners of the originals for permission to reproduce in this edition

Introduction

The first circumnavigation of the globe by a sailing ship was an event much more astonishing to the minds of men in 1522 than, to the modern mind, the first orbiting of the earth by a man-made satellite in 1957. But when Magellan sailed with his fleet of five small ships from the Spanish port of San Lúcar de Barrameda in September 1519 he had not conceived a voyage round the world. By a westward navigation he expected to reach the Moluccas or Spice Islands, which the Portuguese had attained from the Indian Ocean while he was still in their service. Not for the first or last time in the history of discovery, it was the discrepancy between what the venturer expected and what he found that significantly enriched human experience and knowledge. To the world map Magellan added the Pacific Ocean, which occupies one third of the earth's surface, with an area exceeding that of all the land surfaces of the globe. Columbus, at the Isthmus of Panama, thought himself 19 days' journey from the Ganges; for his crossing of the South Pacific Magellan required 98 days. Although the westward passage which he pioneered through the Straits named for him was not to become a regular trade route, he discovered the wind systems which controlled navigation in the South Sea. The reports on the island peoples of the ocean and its archipelagos carried home by the survivors of the expedition opened to the eyes of Europeans a window on a new and strange cultural world. The Portuguese monopoly of information on the eastern seas and on their operations there was broken, and a new factor in the geopolitical rivalry of Spain and Portugal emerged.

If the *Victoria*, the only ship of the five to complete the circumnavigation, had never got back to Spain, few of these momentous consequences – political, economic, scientific – would have followed. From the departure in October 1519 of Magellan's fleet from Tenerife, where they took on additional supplies, until the return of the *Victoria* alone under Juan Sebastián de Elcano, almost exactly three years later, no precise information on the fate and discoveries of the

expedition reached Europe, with the exception of the news carried
to Spain in May 1521 by the *Santo Antonio* which, under Estevão
Gomes, had deserted the fleet in the Straits of Magellan six months
earlier.

   Considered in the light of its influence on the course of history,
the most precious cargo brought back in the *Victoria* was not the
load of cloves in her hold but the information carried in the memories
or notebooks of the eighteen European survivors. This became
immediately available in Spain, and in one form or another – by oral,
written or printed report – a good deal of it was diffused through
other countries. It was not until two years after the *Victoria* moored
at Seville that the testimony collected from those members of the
expedition who had been captured by the Portuguese in the
Moluccas in November 1522 reached Portugal.

The Records of the First Circumnavigation

The essential documents of a sea voyage, recording the course of the
ship and occurrences during the voyage, are the logs or journals of
the commanders, masters, and pilots responsible for her navigation.
Neither Magellan's own journals nor those of the captains who, in
succession, commanded the ships of the fleet have come to light.*
If Elcano, who, in 1519 sailed as master of the *Concepción* and commanded the *Victoria* from August 1521 until her return, kept any
written records, they too have been lost.† His oral testimony to
the events of the voyage is preserved in the report of his examina-
tion at Valladolid on 18 October 1522‡ and in the pages of the
historian Oviedo, who picked his memory. Oral evidence was taken

---

* It is conceivable that Magellan's papers were in the *Trinidad* and either seized
with her by the Portuguese in November 1522 (and subsequently lost) or
destroyed by her commander before his surrender.

† At the inquiry into the voyage held at Valladolid in October 1522, Elcano
stated 'that, while Magellan was alive, he (Elcano) had written nothing, because he dared not do so. That, after he himself was elected captain and treasurer, whatever transactions did take place were recorded.'

‡ This was mainly concerned with the conduct of the fleet and the relations

from survivors of the expedition by the Valladolid commission in 1522 and by the joint Spanish–Portuguese commission, or Junta, of Badajoz-Elvas in 1524. They were also interviewed at Valladolid in 1522 by diplomats and publicists about the Emperor's court, such as Peter Martyr. Documents of the voyage, some now lost, were used by the Spanish historian Antonio de Herrera. The recollections of the men who surrendered at Ternate in November 1522 to António de Brito, the Portuguese governor of the Moluccas, were incorporated in the letter which he wrote to King João III on 6 May 1523; and the papers which de Brito took from them found their way into the Portuguese archives, to be used by the chroniclers Gaspar Corrêa and João de Barros, among others.

The only surviving nautical documents written on the voyage or from memory are a handful of pilots' logs or *derroteros*. The most detailed and informative are those of Francisco Albo, who began the voyage as boatswain in the *Trinidad* and ended it as pilot of the *Victoria*, and of a nameless 'Genoese pilot', identified as Giovanni Battista Punzarol (Poncuron?) or Leone Pancaldo, both of whom were taken prisoner in the *Trinidad* at Ternate. Albo's log was kept as far as the Cape Verde Islands on the return voyage, the Genoese pilot's only as far as the Moluccas. Both record the customary navigational data of winds, courses, distances run, and positions. Other seamen who wrote accounts of the voyage were Ginés de Mafra (who, with Pancaldo, was among the only four men of the *Trinidad* to return to Spain) and three anonymous pilots or sailors.

It is in other sources than the professional records of seamen that we find, besides details of navigation, the observations of people, countries and events which clothe with flesh the skeleton of the voyage and breathe life into its dramatic story. Peter Martyr, the Italian humanist who, during his long residence at the Spanish court, became 'the earliest historian of America' and of the great discoveries, had excellent opportunities for gathering authentic

between its senior officers, on which Pigafetta says very little. He was not called to give evidence at the inquiry.

information from the mouths of the venturers. Ramusio, in 1550, recorded that 'the voyage [of Magellan and the *Victoria*] was described very minutely by Peter Martyr . . . But, as it was sent to be printed in Rome, it was lost in the miserable sacking of that city [in 1527]; and nothing is known even now as to where it is.'★

The earliest printed narrative of the circumnavigation was compiled by the same processes as the lost 'history' of Peter Martyr. This was the letter, dated from Valladolid 22 October 1522, addressed to his father, the Cardinal-Archbishop of Salzburg, by Maximilian of Transylvania, a pupil of Peter Martyr and secretary to the Emperor, who had married a niece of Cristóbal de Haro, the principal investor in Magellan's enterprise. As the date of the letter indicates, Maximilian had his information from Elcano and his two companions, Francisco Albo and Hernando de Bustamante, who were then in Valladolid, and to their recollections it plainly owes the freshness of the observations recorded in it. As a courtier and a man of sophisticated intelligence, with connections in the corridors of power, Maximilian also made a serious attempt to display the circumnavigation against the background of politics and diplomacy in the Far East.

But the longest and most valuable narrative of the voyage was written by a young Italian who was neither a professional seaman nor a humanist. Antonio Pigafetta, who, joining the expedition as a volunteer, was in the *Trinidad* when she sailed in 1519 and in the *Victoria* when she berthed in 1522, brought to his task of recording a capacity for keen observation, sympathetic interpretation, and expressive communication of experience which enabled him to produce one of the most remarkable documents in the history of geographical and ethnological discovery. His Relation contains the testimony of an independent witness, disengaged from the processes by which other reports of the expedition were transmitted through Spanish or Portuguese official channels or through the minds and pens of literary men. Without Pigafetta's account, the knowledge of the

★ G. B. Ramusio, *Navigationi*.

peoples of the Pacific and their way of life won by the experience of the voyagers would, in large part, never have been conveyed to Europe.

Antonio Pigafetta and His Relation

The earlier life of Antonio Pigafetta, before he arrived in Spain and joined Megallan's expedition as a supernumerary in 1519, is obscure and undocumented. He came of a noble family of Vicenza and could therefore claim Venetian citizenship. Statements of the date of his birth, made by later writers, vary between 1480 and 1491; it seems likely that, when he made the circumnavigation, he was nearer thirty than forty years of age, and the later birth date is more persuasive. In addressing his narrative of the voyage to the Grand Master of Rhodes in (probably) the first half of 1525, Pigafetta describes himself as 'patrician of Vicenza and Knight of Rhodes'. Whether he joined the Order of St John of Jerusalem before or after the circumnavigation remains an open question. On a balance of probabilities, it appears reasonable to suppose that he was already a Knight of the Order when he accompanied the papal ambassador to the court of Spain at the end of 1518.

As a Military Knight, Pigafetta would have taken part in the guerrilla warfare at sea waged by the 'Christian corsairs' of Rhodes against the infidel Turks in the Mediterranean. He cannot have been without sea service, even if only in galleys and perhaps not under sail; and he had evidently learned the practice of keeping a journal at sea, though his knowledge of astronomical navigation was very slight. If his explanations of sea matters – for example a ship's rigging and sails, or watches and signals at sea – sometimes seem naive, this was perhaps to make them intelligible to certain of his readers. Allusions or analogies in his narrative suggest that he was familiar from personal experience with both the eastern and the western Mediterranean. Nor was he unlettered, for he read travel books in preparation for the voyage; and his Relation, as eventually written, testifies to this. The strict rules of a militant order would have accustomed him to discipline and inured him to hardship. The experience of the circumnavigation reveals him as a man of strong and fixed loyalties, avid curiosity, and an exceptional capacity for assimilating observed facts, which was sharpened rather than blunted by a certain simplicity of character. He displayed another quality important in a recorder, namely a remarkable faculty for survival.

The Knights of Rhodes, under their Grand Master, owed allegiance only to the Pope and were liable to diplomatic or similar duties in his service. It may have been thus that in 1518 Pigafetta was in the entourage of the Venetian-born protonotary Francesco Chieregati dispatched by Pope Leo X on an embassy to the young King Charles V of Spain, who was to be elected Emperor in June 1519. In January 1519 the ambassador, with Pigafetta in attendance, followed the Spanish court from Zaragoza to Barcelona, which Charles entered on 15 February. It was eleven months since the king had approved the proposals of Magellan and Ruy Faleiro and signed the necessary orders for an expedition under their command to sail 'by the way of the west' and to discover 'that which until now has not been found within our demarcation'. In spite of Portuguese intrigues, the fitting out of the five ships at Seville was now far advanced, and the administrative preparations were expedited by a series of royal *cédulas* issued at Barcelona from March to May 1519, culminating in detailed instructions for the conduct of the voyage. At court Pigafetta heard much talk of the enterprise, listening (as he tells us) to the 'clerks and learned men who discussed the great and terrible things of the Ocean Sea' with his master the protonotary. Among these men was doubtless Pietro Martire d'Anghiera (Peter Martyr), secretary to the king and protonotary of the Council of the Indies. With their encouragement, and (as he says) prompted by a craving for experience and for glory, Pigafetta obtained permission from the king and from his master to volunteer for the voyage, and in May he travelled by sea to Malaga and overland to Seville. There he was mustered in the complement of Magellan's flagship, the *Trinidad*, among the *criados del capitán y sobresalientes* (captain's servants and soldier-supernumeraries, or marines), his name appearing in the registers variously as Antonio de Plegafetis and Antonio Lombardo.

Pigafetta's duties on board ship doubtless left him leisure for writing a daily journal and gathering information ashore on the lands and islands visited by the expedition. The use he made of his opportunities, and the peculiar qualities of the narrative which resulted, are discussed later. Here we need comment only briefly on his personal participation in the events of the voyage. Although fired by a passionate admiration for Magellan, to whom he pays moving homage after the captain-general's death in the Philippines, and by unexplained animosity toward Elcano, who is not mentioned once in his Relation, Pigafetta displays considerable detachment both from the conduct of the expedition and from the persistent conflicts provoked by ill feeling between the Spanish and Portuguese elements in its command. From him, for instance, we learn little about the mutiny at Port St Julian, an event of crucial significance in the voyage.* His success in dealing with indigenous peoples, however, made him useful to the commanders in ceremonial visits, negotiations or trade relations, as when, in January 1522, he was sent ashore on Timor alone by Elcano 'to speak to the chief man . . . that he might give us provisions'. Time and again it was Pigafetta who was chosen for such missions, which (luckily for the historian) gave him occasion to exercise his talent in observing the manners and customs of the local people. When it came to fighting, too, he was well forward, and in the confused struggle on Mactan he was one of the few men to stand by Magellan until ordered to retire by the wounded captain-general.

In tracing the course taken by the ships, Pigafetta, with his slender knowledge of navigation, furnishes less continuous and reliable evidence than the pilots' logs. Nevertheless, his steadfastness and tenacity produced a record which enables us to see the voyage as a whole. It is the more fortunate that, starting the voyage in the flagship, he completed it in the only ship that found its way back to Spain. He was mustered in the *Trinidad* some time between

* See p. 47.

the date in May 1519 when he arrived in Seville and the sailing of
the fleet from San Lúcar on 20 September; and he remained in her
until the death of Magellan on 27 April 1521, after that under the
command of Duarte Barbosa until the massacre at Cebu on 1 May
(which Pigafetta escaped by remaining on board to nurse a wound
received at Mactan), and thereafter, in succession, under João
Carvalho and Gonzalo Gómez de Espinosa. When, at Tidore, the
Trinidad had to be left behind for repair and her sole remaining
consort the *Victoria* parted company on 21 December 1521, Pigafetta
was not among those who 'wished to remain there for fear that she
could not . . . go all the way to Spain' or 'for fear of dying of
hunger'; and he transferred to Elcano's command in the *Victoria*.
So he was one of the eighteen men, 'leaner than an old worn out
hack',⋆ who, on 9 September 1522, the day after reaching Seville,
'went, in our shirts and barefoot, and each with a torch in his hand,
to visit the shrine of Santa Maria de la Victoria' to give thanks for
their safe return.

Very soon after this Pigafetta made his way to Valladolid where,
before 21 October, he had an interview with the Emperor. His subsequent journeyings, between October 1522 and August 1524, took
him to Lisbon, to France, to Mantua, to his home in Vicenza, to
Venice, to Rome by way of Viterbo and Monterosi (where he had
his meetings with the Grand Master), and back to Venice.

During this time he was composing his Relation of the voyage
and preparing copies of it; and, as part of the story of its transmission, his movements in this period are described in more detail in
the next section. On 3 October 1524 he was granted the benefice of
Norcia, in the gift of the Order of St John, for which he had sued on
25 July. There is some reason to suppose that the copy of the Relation which he designed for the Grand Master, and from which all the
surviving manuscripts derive, was completed and presented between January and June 1525. Of the remainder of Pigafetta's life
nothing certain is known. Rumour or conjecture recorded by later
writers affirms that he was fighting against the Turks in 1536, after

⋆ The phrase is Peter Martyr's.

the loss of Tunis, and then retired to Vicenza, or (alternatively) that he died at Malta in 1534 or 1535. No documentation supports these stories or gives the authentic date of Pigafetta's death.

In the Prologue to his Relation, Pigafetta writes that he decided, with the approval of the Emperor and of Monsignor Chieregati, 'to experience and to go to see some of the said things [of the ocean sea], thereby to satisfy the wishes of the said lords and also mine own'. This might be taken to mean that Pigafetta was attached to Magellan's expedition in the capacity (so the speak) of a special correspondent commissioned to bring back a report of the voyage, either to the court of Spain or to the Venetian authorities. The interpretation may be far fetched, even if after his return Pigafetta was to talk freely in various quarters about his experiences. Indisputably, however, he was from the outset aware of his responsibility as an eyewitness of 'great and marvellous things' and prepared himself to make a record of them for eventual communication or publication. We have implicit testimony to his intention. That he began to keep a journal from the departure of the fleet, and maintained it throughout the voyage, is shown by the consistent fullness and detail in his descriptions of things seen from beginning to end of the narrative, with regular noting of dates. The supply of writing paper on board was sufficient to allow some of it to be used as gifts to the king and notables of Brunei. Pigafetta carried a notebook about with him, and the King of Limasawa, in the Philippines, was 'astonished' to see him writing down 'many things as they call them in their language'. Apart from the vocabularies, the particularity of detail in many of Pigafetta's descriptions and anecdotes could only have come from well-stocked notebooks, entered on the spot or immediately after his return to the ship.

As a chronicle of the voyage, the Relation has some obvious limitations. The track of the ships could not be laid down from Pigafetta's entries of data relating to navigation, which are not continuously logged, are often incorrect or garbled (either in communication from the pilots who supplied them or in subsequent transmission), and are sometimes teasingly vague. Occasionally, as in the Plate estuary, he streamlines the course of events. When he writes a note on Magellan's correction of the compasses for local magnetic declination after leaving the Straits, or on the Southern Cross and 'Magellanic clouds', or on the estimation of the ship's speed through the water, the explanation is so oversimplified as to be barely intelligible to the reader, and perhaps also (we may guess) to the writer.

Pigafetta evidently put into his notebooks whatever he heard as well as what he saw. If, in consequence, the Relation transmits a good many tall stories and unverified or ill-digested information, we need not complain. Herodotus, like Pigafetta, could affirm that 'I report that which I am told, but I am not obliged to believe it all alike'; nor are his readers. But Pigafetta was no Mandeville, spinning tales of travel from the geographical books in his study; and it is only rarely that his reading leaves traces in the Relation. Where he records hearsay, it is that of the inhabitants whom he encountered on shore in the Philippines, Borneo, the Moluccas and the Sunda Islands, or of the native pilots taken on board after leaving the Philippines and in Tidore. These pilots, presumed to be Javanese, could not only give him more precise information about Java and the neighbouring islands than any yet available in Europe; they had in the course of their business navigated up and down the eastern seas and could, from talk on nautical matters with other seamen in ports where they congregated, also tell Pigafetta about countries, coasts, harbours, and trade routes even beyond their own range. So he heard, and wrote down, much that is of little less interest today than it was to his contemporary readers about the countries of the Bay of Bengal, the Malayan peninsula, and Indochina, and especially about 'China the Great, the king of which is the greatest in all the world'.

With neither the pilots nor (more significantly) the people of the islands visited does Pigafetta complain of any difficulty in communication; it was sometimes by signs, more commonly through the Malay interpreter Enrique of Malacca★ or (we must suppose) in

★ Until his death at Cebu in May 1521.

direct if halting conversation. As Professor Lach observes, 'it would seem that, by the time he left the archipelago, Pigafetta had acquired a working knowledge of two of the most important dialects of the Indonesian languages', namely Bisayan and Malay; and (he adds) 'the question as to how he was able to get this vocabulary [*i.e.* the the list of 450 Malay words] together during his short stay in the East Indies has perplexed many students of Pigafetta's work'.* Pigafetta gives a few hints of his method, as when, 'with pen in hand', he asked the Patagonian giant in the *Trinidad* for words in his tongue (Tehuelche) which he wrote down 'quickly', or when he took down Bisayan words at the court of the King of Limasawa. The facility with which modern philologists have identified many of the words in Pigafetta's vocabularies of the Tupi or Guarani, Tehuelche, Bisayan and Malay languages, and the identifiable phonetic forms in which he renders indigenous place names, suggest that he had an excellent ear. To this may be added the particular aptitude he exhibited for dealing sympathetically with the inhabitants of the lands or islands discovered and (arising from this) the fact that, while in the Pacific, he probably spent more time ashore than any other member of the expedition.

Pigafetta's lively interest in people, supported by his linguistic aptitude, enabled him to absorb, like a sponge, an altogether re-markable quantity of information. This embraced not only visible evidence of the way of life in the indigenous communities which he encountered – for instance, their food production and preparation, their clothing (or lack of it) and weapons, the manners of their daily life (eating, sleeping, sexual habits, ceremonial, and so on), their houses and boats, their methods of trade and barter. It extended also to matters which could (in part, at least) only have been gathered by oral communication, such as the political relationship between native kingdoms, their social stratification and polity, their com-mercial network with distant countries, and the religious faith of the people.

The framework of the Relation is a narrative constructed by

* Donald F. Lach, *Asia in the making of Europe.*

Pigafetta from the daily entries of his journal; but into this are inter-
polated a series of discursive accounts of the places and peoples
which came under his notice, compiled no doubt from his notebooks.
There are the descriptions of the Tupi or Guarani Indians of Brazil,
of the Tehuelche of Patagonia, and of the Micronesian islanders of
the Marianas – all relatively superficial for lack of direct communication. There are elaborate and highly detailed accounts of life on
three of the Philippine Islands (Suluan, Limasawa, Cebu), in Palawan
and Brunei, and in Tidore. When Magellan's expedition reached these
islands, none of them had yet been visited by the Portuguese. For
the geography and history of the pre-Spanish Philippines, Pigafetta's account is a primary source, objective and sympathetic. For
the history of Borneo, 'the European sources . . . have importance
. . . because there are almost no native annals or monuments of so
early a date to tell of the island's past'; among these sources Pigafetta's Relation is the earliest of substance and reliability. The com-
plex political situation in the Moluccas, and (more significantly)
the cultivation and marketing of the spices, are described by Pigafetta with a fullness and precision which gave his account authority
throughout the sixteenth century. On the social, political and religious circumstances of the Pacific communities with which the men
of Magellan's expedition were brought into contact, Pigafetta's
Relation must still be consulted by ethnologists and historians of
today. The public of his own time, however, or indeed for nearly
three hundred years thereafter, had no opportunity of reading the
Relation in full, as he wrote it and designed it for publication.

If any charts were drawn by the pilots during the circumnavigation they have disappeared. The cartographic sketches, twenty-three
in number, which illustrate the extant manuscripts of Pigafetta's
Relation, must be derived from originals executed during the
voyage. Their simplicity of character points to the work of an un-
professional hand, most probably Pigafetta's. The orientation, with
south to the top, and the style of coastal drawing, strongly remini-
scent of contemporary *isolarii* or island atlases of the Mediterranean,
suggest that he followed the pattern of cartographic works familiar

to him. However conventional, the little charts are the only first-hand graphic materials to survive from the circumnavigation.

The Transmission of Pigafetta's Relation

Pigafetta's statement that he entered his journal daily may be accepted as substantially, if not literally, true. His remarkable pertinacity and regularity in logging each day's events enabled him to detect, at the Cape Verde Islands, the 'loss' of a day by the Spaniards on their circumnavigation in a westerly direction. The daily journal and the notebooks kept by him, which have not survived, were the raw material from which he compiled accounts of the voyage for presentation to notable persons and for publication.

After the *Victoria* tied up at the Mole of Seville on 8 September 1522 (how long after is unknown), Pigafetta hastened to the Spanish court at Valladolid, independently of his commander Elcano, who was summoned by the Emperor on 13 September and appeared in October with two companions, Albo the pilot and Bustamante the barber, before a court of inquiry into the voyage. At Valladolid Pigafetta (as he records) presented to the Emperor, as something to be prized above gold and silver, 'a book written by my hand treating of all the things that had occurred day by day on our voyage'. There seems no reason to doubt, with some historians, that this gift was a written account, not a merely oral one, abstracted doubtless from Pigafetta's journal; if so, this too has not been preserved.

Pigafetta may still have been at Valladolid on 21 October, when the Mantuan ambassador Antonio Bagarotto reported in a letter to Isabella d'Este, mother of the reigning Marquis Federigo II Gonzaga, that the survivors of Magellan's expedition had brought back 'a very beautiful book containing an account of their voyage and the countries which they had visited'; and on 21 November the ambassador sent to Mantua extracts from, or a summary of, the book. At Valladolid, too, Pigafetta may have talked to Peter Martyr and his young pupil Maximilian of Transylvania, although the latter seems to have had his information mainly from Elcano and his companions.

The traveller went on to Lisbon, where King João III received an oral report from him, and to France, where he gave the Queen Mother, Louise of Savoy, 'some things from the other hemisphere'.

As a consequence of Bagarotto's reports and (it seems) with a recommendation from his former master Francesco Chieregati, who had seen the manuscript presented to the Emperor, Pigafetta next appears in February or March 1523 at the court of Mantua, where he undertook to compose for Federigo Gonzaga a formal narrative of the voyage from his papers. At this task he worked in his home at Vicenza during 1523, interrupted by a visit in November to Venice, where the diarist Marino Sanudo recorded the reception of 'a gentleman of Vicenza called the knight errant, a brother of [the Order of] Rhodes, who has been three years in India', by the Doge and Signory. After his return to Vicenza, he received an imperative summons to Rome from the new Pope, Clement VII. On the road thither (as he relates), at the little town of Monterosi between Viterbo and Rome, he encountered the Grand Master of the Order of St John, Philippe de Villiers l'Isle-Adam, who had retired to Italy after the siege and surrender of Rhodes in 1522. To him also he narrated the tale of his voyage and promised a written relation. Pigafetta's reception by the Pope, with whom he left written notes and drawings, was encouraging. He was given assurance of a licence to print his book, and on 2 February 1524 he wrote to the Marquis of Mantua promising him the first printed copy. In Rome Pigafetta must have finished the writing of his book, but by April he seems to have abandoned hope of papal patronage and was applying to enter Mantuan service. In August, back in Venice, he addressed to the Doge and Senate a petition (which was to be granted) reciting that he, 'Antonio Pigafetta, Venetian Knight of Jerusalem', had 'circumnavigated the whole world and . . . composed a short narration of all the said voyage', for which, desiring to print it, he requested a copyright privilege for twenty years. The complete manuscript of his narration was, however, not published by Pigafetta (perhaps for lack of funds) or by anyone else during the sixteenth century.

The documents from which this account of Pigafetta's movements is constructed refer to only four manuscript accounts from his papers which came into other hands before or after he arrived in Mantua early in 1523. The first was the 'book' which he gave to the Emperor in September 1522, doubtless (for want of time) a summary rapidly compiled from his journal; a copy perhaps taken from Valladolid to Nuremberg before 26 December 1522; extracts forwarded to Mantua on 12 November 1522; and the papers, including drawings, given to the Pope in January 1524. None of these manuscripts is known to have survived. There is no evidence that, before his arrival in Mantua, he had either begun to write a formal Relation or presented copies of his journal or other manuscripts to João III, to Louise of Savoy, or to anyone else, apart from the Emperor. The assertion by some editors that, on his passage through France, he gave Queen Louise 'some sort of a copy . . . of his journal' rests on a strained interpretation of Pigafetta's reference to 'some things from the other hemisphere' and on some equivocal statements, probably both by Ramusio, in Italian versions of the Relation printed in 1536 and 1550.

There can be little doubt that the composition of the Relation, in the form transmitted by the surviving manuscripts, began in March 1523 and that Pigafetta continued to work at it in Mantua, Vicenza and Rome, where he probably completed it by April 1524. All four extant manuscripts of the Relation contain the dedication to the Grand Master of Rhodes, so styled. After the fall of Rhodes, the Grand Master transferred the headquarters of the Order to Italy, and from 25 January 1524 until January 1527 it was at Viterbo, though Villiers de l'Isle-Adam was out of Italy after 25 June 1525. The Order was established in succession at Corneto, from January to August 1527, and at Nice until 1530, when, under letters patent from the Emperor, the Knights occupied Malta. If the dedication copy of Pigafetta's Relation was presented to the 'Grand Master of Rhodes' in Italy, as its last sentence suggests, this was certainly before July 1529 and probably before June 1525, at Viterbo. Pigafetta's application, on 25 July 1524, for a *commenda* or benefice in the gift of the Order and his investiture with the benefice of Norcia, on 3 October, might seem to narrow the date bracket still more, if the presentation of his manuscript were designed to support his petition or to express his gratitude. But the designation of Louise of Savoy as 'Regent' (in all manuscripts) can only refer to the period between February 1525 (battle of Pavia) and January 1526 (treaty of Madrid).

The fact that, of the four extant manuscripts, one is in the Venetian dialect of Italian and three are in French implies that they were prepared for different patrons, as indeed the textual evidence suggests. If all four were executed in Pigafetta's lifetime, if not at his instance, it is curiously inconsistent with contemporary practice that each of them has the same dedication, which doubtless stood in the Grand Master's original presentation copy or in Pigafetta's draft for it. The language in which he wrote his Relation is a question vigorously debated by editors for over a century and a half, in terms which need not be recited here. There are in fact three questions. Was Italian or French the language of (a) his own draft and (b) the manuscript presented to the Grand Master, and (c) what is the textual relationship between the extant Italian manuscript and the three French manuscripts? As to the first question, apart from the facts that Italian was Pigafetta's native language and that two surviving holograph letters of Pigafetta show 'an almost perfect identity of style and language' with the Italian manuscript of the Relation, chronology lends strong support to the belief that the original draft was written in Italian. It is at the instance of the Gonzaga ruling family, in Mantua, that he begins to write. By the time, nearly a year later, that he meets the Grand Master at Monterosi, his draft must have been well advanced; and some eight months later he obtains a privilege for printing his book in Venice. These simple considerations remove any serious doubt that Pigafetta had, by August 1524, written the original version of his book for publication in Italian.

The question of the Grand Master's presentation copy, and of the language in which it was written, is more open-ended. This copy

Introduction

was certainly not the rather tatty Italian manuscript in the Biblioteca Ambrosiana. It has been argued that, since the Grand Master was a Frenchman and the official language of the Knights of St John was French, it must have been in that language that the presentation copy was written. This hypothesis presents certain difficulties. The correctness of style in the French manuscripts excludes the possibility of their redaction by Pigafetta himself; yet it is clear, from the wording in the Relation and from the chronology outlined above, that the manuscript for presentation to the Grand Master was prepared in Italy and (with some probability) before June 1525. Nor do the textual divergences between the extant French and Italian manuscripts, some of them of an editorial character, indicate that Pigafetta need have had a hand in correcting or revising the French versions.

The Italian manuscript in the Biblioteca Ambrosiana, Milan, may be described as workmanlike rather than elegant. Written on paper in a neat humanistic hand, unilluminated, and illustrated by twenty-three map-sketches, it is nevertheless the only remaining representative of the textual tradition deriving from Pigafetta's original draft and thus supplies a useful datum for interpretation or emendation of the French versions. Two of the French manuscripts are in the Bibliothèque Nationale, Paris: firstly, a plainly written paper manuscript, which came into the royal library in 1694, and secondly, more finely written and illuminated manuscript on vellum, though with considerable abridgment of the text. The third and most complete French manuscript is the Nancy-Libri-Phillipps-Beinecke-Yale codex, here translated, which is certainly the most magnificent of the four manuscripts in respect of its writing, its illumination, and its maps. It is not possible to ascribe a precise date to the writing of any of the French manuscripts; that they are all early, that is, executed within few years after Pigafetta's original draft, has not been seriously disputed. Collation of the texts suggests that each of the three manuscripts derives from a common source in a (lost) French text translated from the Italian, with some editorial manipulation.

Comparison of the two best French manuscripts leaves little doubt of the textual superiority of the Beinecke-Yale codex. It has a few scribal errors peculiar to itself, occasional phrases are unhappily reworded, and there is a good deal of superficial editing, in the interests of style or intelligibility, by insertion of neutral linking phrases or of explanations. In the great majority of cases where these two manuscripts disagree, however, the reading of the Beinecke-Yale is supported by that of the Ambrosiana manuscript and may thus be supposed to reproduce more faithfully Pigafetta's own text.

A Note on the Translation

That this is the first rendering of the entire French text into English has determined the method of translation and annotation adopted. So far as possible, the English version attempts to reproduce the characteristic flavour and vocabulary of the original text written down in the early sixteenth century by an Italian soldier unpractised in literary composition, though endowed with a curious temper and an acute visual sense which lend vitality and movement to his narrative. Pigafetta's prose has no elegance of construction or rhythm; it bursts from him in a succession of rather breathless short sentences. His vocabulary is homely, without sophistication or scholarship. It is hoped that the present translation will communicate to the English reader the impression of naivety and spontaneity, in style and form, made by the original text, yet without serious loss of intelligibility. Its punctuation and sentence division have, in general, been followed, as have the linking of sentences by particles and Pigafetta's somewhat unsystematic use of the past and present tenses.

The vocabulary of the translation has been assimilated to that of sixteenth century English. For Italian and French measures, approximate English equivalents have (where possible) been substituted, e.g. for *brasse* (*braza*), cubit or fathom. Names of European persons, places, and ships have been rendered in the accepted modern form, and so have descriptive place names bestowed by Magellan or his men; but indigenous words (e.g. *capac, picis*) and names of persons or places (e.g. Raia Humabon, Mazzaua, Zzubu) are reproduced in the orthography of the French manuscript. Terms of modern origin have been avoided; thus *le more* in the original is translated 'the Moor', not 'the Moro'.

R. A. SKELTON

A Note on this Edition

The edition of *Magellan's Voyage* published by the Yale University Press in 1969 originally appeared in two volumes, the second consisting of a facsimile of the Beinecke manuscript. In this edition, the translation of Pigafetta's text is reproduced in full with only minor emendations, but those parts of the Introduction that dealt with a detailed description of the Beinecke manuscript or with a comparison between it and the other surviving manuscripts, together with a few passages mainly related to supplementary sources, have been omitted. Notes to those sources, as well as notes on variorum readings, have also been deleted. Five of the illustrations are taken from the facsimile volume.

NAVI GATION·ET

descouurement de la Inde
superieure, et isles de Malucque, ou
naissent les cloux de Girofle. faic̄ Le par
Anthoine Pigaphete vincentin Cheuallier de Rhodes.
Com
manceant en
lan Mil v .cc. et xix

Anthoyne Pigaphete Patricie Vincentin et Cheuallier de
Rhodes. a Illustrissme et tres excellent Seigneur Philippe de Villers
L'Isleadam inclite grand Maistre de Rhodes son seigneur osseruanissme.

,NEAGECITO,

Navigation and discovery of

Upper India and the Isles of Molucca,

where the cloves grow.

Made by

Antonio Pigafetta of Vicenza,

Knight of Rhodes.

Beginning in the year

MDXIX.

Antonio Pigafetta, patrician of Vicenza and Knight of Rhodes, to the most illustrious and very excellent Lord Philippe de Villiers l'Isle-Adam, renowned Grand Master of Rhodes, his most honoured lord.

NE AGE CITO, 'hasten not', an anagram of JEAN COGNET, the earliest known owner of the manuscript.

CHAPTER I

Prologue of Antonio Pigafetta to his present book treating of the navigation to the Molucca Islands, of Fernão de Magalhães, captain-general of the fleet that made the voyage, and of the hatred which the masters and other captains bore to him.

Forasmuch as (most illustrious and very reverend Lord) there are divers curious persons who not only take pleasure in hearing and knowing the great and marvellous things which God has permitted me to see and suffer during the long and perilous voyage which I have made, hereafter written, but who also wish to know the means and fashion and the road which I took to go thither, not lending faith or firm belief to the end until they are first informed and assured of the beginning: wherefore, my Lord, be pleased to understand that, finding myself in Spain, in the year of the Nativity of our Lord 1519, at the court of the most serene King of the Romans,* with the reverend Monsignor, master Francesco Chieregati, then apostolic protonotary and ambassador of Pope Leo X (and who has since by his virtue attained to the bishopric of Aprutino and principality of Teramo), and having learned, both by reading of divers books and from the report of many clerks and learned men who discussed the great and terrible things of the Ocean Sea with the said protonotary, I determined (by the good favour of the Emperor and the above-mentioned lord) to experience and to go to see some of the said things, thereby to satisfy the wishes of the said lords and also mine, that it might be told that I made the voyage and saw with my eyes the things hereafter written, and that I might win a famous name with posterity.

Now, to come to unfold the beginning of my voyage (most illustrious lord) having heard that there was in the city of Seville a small

* Charles V, King of Spain; elected Emperor in June 1519. Chieregati, with Pigafetta in attendance, had in January 1519 followed Charles's court from Zaragoza to Barcelona. As Pigafetta arrived in Seville three months before Magellan's preparations were completed (by 10 August), he must have left Barcelona early in May.

fleet to the number of five ships★ ready to make that long voyage, that is, to find and discover the isles of Molucca whence come the spices (of which fleet the captain-general was Fernão de Magalhães, a Portuguese gentleman, commander of the Order of Santiago de la Spada,† who had made several voyages in the Ocean Sea in which he had deported himself honourably and as a man of worth), I set out with several letters of recommendation from Barcelona, where at that time the Emperor was, and came by sea to Malaga. And from the sea I went by land until I reached the above-mentioned city of Seville, where I abode the space of three months waiting for the said fleet to be put in order and prepared for its voyage. And inasmuch (most illustrious lord) as on my return from the voyage, going to Rome to visit our Holy Father‡ I found your lordship at Monterosi where of your grace you made me welcome and later gave me to understand that you desired to have in writing the things which God by his grace allowed me to see in my said voyage: therefore to satisfy and yield to your wish I have set down in this little book the principal things as best I could. Finally (most illustrious lord), all preparations having been made and the ships put in order, the captain-general, a wise and virtuous man and mindful of his honour, would not begin his voyage without first issuing some good and honourable regulations, as it is the good custom to make for those who go to sea. But he did not wholly declare the voyage which he wished to make, lest the people from astonishment and fear refuse to accompany him on so long a voyage as he had in mind to undertake, in view of the great and violent storms of the Ocean Sea whither he would go.§ And for another reason also. For the masters and cap-

★ The five ships were: *Santo Antonio, Trinidad, Concepción, Victoria* and *Santiago.* The *Trinidad,* flying Magellan's pennant, was *capitana* or flagship of the fleet.
† As a mark of favour to the expedition, Charles had in July 1518 decorated Magellan and Ruy Faleiro with the cross of *comendador* of the Order of Santiago.
‡ Pope Clement VII, elected 19 November 1523. Pigafetta, passing through Monterosi where he met the Grand Master, was in Rome by December 1523 or January 1524.
§ The charts prepared for the voyage were not issued to the captains and

tains of the other ships of his company loved him not. I do not know the reason, unless it be that he, the captain-general, was Portuguese, and they were Spaniards or Castilians, which peoples have long borne ill-will and malevolence toward one another.★ Notwithstanding, they all held obedience to him and he made his regulations as follows, that in the hazards of the sea (which often occur by night and by day) the ships should not go astray and separate from each other. Which regulations he published and issued in writing to each ship's master, and ordered that they be observed and kept inviolably, unless with great and legitimate excuse and evidence of being unable to do otherwise.

CHAPTER II

Regulations made by the captain-general for the conduct of his ships, their watches by night, and gathering of his fleet.

𝔍irst, the said captain-general desired that the ship in which he was should go before the other ships and that the others should follow him; and to this end he carried by night on the poop of his ship a torch or burning fagot of wood, which they called *farol*, that his ships should not lose him from sight. Sometimes he put a lantern, at other times a thick cord of lighted rushes, called *trenche*, which was made of rushes soaked in water and beaten, then dried in the sun or by smoke. And this was a thing very favourable for the

★ Of the other captains, Juan de Cartagena (*S. Antonio*), Gaspar Quesada (*Concepción*), and Luis de Mendoza (*Victoria*) were Spanish; only João Serrão (*Santiago*) was Portuguese. Of the masters (warrant officers in charge of the crew), two were Basque and three Italian. The pilots, whom Pigafetta does not mention in this connection, were all Portuguese: Estevão Gomes (*Trinidad*). João Rodrigues de Mafra (*S. Antonio*), João Lopes Carvalho (*Concepción*), Vasco Gallego (*Victoria*), and João Serrão (*Santiago*). The total complement of the ships, 270–280 men, included at least 37 Portuguese.

pilots until the fleet had put to sea from the Guadalquivir; nor was the objective of the expedition, the Moluccas, marked on them.

purpose. When the captain had made one of his signals to the people, they responded to him likewise. Thus he knew whether the ships were following him or not. And when he wished to change course because the weather changed, or the wind was contrary, or he wanted to reduce way, he had two lights shown. And if he wished the others to haul in a bonnet (which is a part of the sail attached to the main sail)* he showed three lights. Thus by three lights, even if the weather was good for sailing faster, he meant that the said bonnet be brought in, so that the mainsail could be sooner and more easily struck and furled when bad weather came on suddenly in some squall or otherwise. Likewise, when the captain wished the other ships to strike sail, he showed four lights, which he quickly caused to be extinguished. Then he showed one as a signal that he wished to stop there and remain, so that the other ships did as he. Further, when he discovered some land or reef (that is, a rock in the sea) he showed several lights, or fired a mortar once. And if he wished to make sail, he signalled to the other ships by four lights, that they should do as he and follow him. And he always kept the aforesaid *farol* hanging at the poop of his ship. Also when he wished to lace the bonnet on the sail again, he showed three lights. And to know also whether all the ships were following him and coming together he showed only one light besides the *farol*. And then each of the ships showed another light in reply.

Besides the above-mentioned regulations, to practise the art of the sea (as is customary) and to avoid the dangers which may befall those who do not set watches, the said lieutenant, expert in matters of navigation, ordered three watches to be set at night: the first at the beginning of the night, the second at midnight, and the third toward daybreak, commonly called the *diane*, otherwise the [watch

* The bonnet was a narrow rectangular sail laced to the foot of the course (foresail, mainsail, or mizzen); two were commonly fitted below the mainsail. Sail was shortened by lowering the yard and unlacing, or 'shaking off' a bonnet, and increased by 'lacing on' a bonnet and raising the yard. Pigafetta's parenthetic explanation of this nautical term is typically naive.

of the] morning star. And every night the said watches were changed, that is to say, he who had made the first watch made on the morrow the second, and he who had made the second then made the third. And after this manner they changed every night. Then the captain ordered that his regulations, both for signals and for watches, be strictly observed, that their voyage be made with greater safety. The people of the fleet were divided into three companies: the first was the captain's, the second that of the pilot or boatswain's mate, the third that of the master.★ The said regulations being made, the captain-general prepared to sail, as related below.

CHAPTER III

The departure of the five ships from the port of Seville. Of the river called Betis. The dangers which there are in navigating it. Of the place San Lucar. And the sojourn which the captain-general made along the river Betis, now called Guadalquivir.

On Monday, St Lawrence's day, the tenth of August in the aforesaid year, the fleet, having been furnished with all that was necessary for it, and having in the five ships people of divers nations to the number of two hundred and thirty-seven in all,† was ready to depart from the Mole of Seville,‡ and firing all the artillery we set sail with the staysail only and came to the mouth of a river named

---

★ The executive officers of a Spanish ship in order of precedence, with approximate English equivalents, were the captain, the pilot, the master (*maestre*), the boatswain (*contramaestre*), and the boatswain's mate (*nochiero*).
† This is the number of persons who received four months' advance pay, but at least 268 men actually embarked. Difficulties in recruiting perhaps explain the medley of nationalities, for, besides Spaniards, Portuguese and Basques, there were Genoese, Sicilians, French, Flemings, Germans, Greeks, Neapolitans, Corfiotes, Negroes and Malays. All the gunners, of which each ship carried three, were foreigners, generally French, but sometimes Germans or Flemings. The *Trinidad*'s master gunner was Master Andrew of Bristol, the only Englishman, who had married a woman of Seville.
‡ The Puerto de las Muelas, in Seville harbour.

Betis, which is now called Guadalquivir. And going by this river we passed by a place named Gioan de Farax where there was a great settlement of Moors.* And there was there a bridge over the river by which one went to Seville, which bridge was in ruins, although two columns remained at the bottom of the water. Wherefore you must have practised and expert men of the country to point out the proper channel for passing safely between these two columns, for fear of striking on them. Further, it is necessary to pass the bridge and other parts of the said river when the water is fairly high. After passing the two columns we arrived at a place named Coria. And passing through several small villages along the river, at length we arrived at a castle belonging to the Duke of Medina Sidonia called San Lucar, which is a port by which to enter the Ocean Sea.† You enter it on the west wind and depart from it on the east wind. And nearby is Cape St Vincent, which (according to the cosmography) lies in thirty-seven degrees of latitude and twenty miles distant from the said port.‡ And from the city to the port by the afore-mentioned river there are thirty-five or forty miles. A few days after, the captain-general went along the said river in his boat, and the masters of the other ships with him, and we remained for some days at the port to supply the fleet with some necessary things. We went every day to hear mass on land at a church named Our Lady of Barrameda near San Lucar, where the captain ordered all those of the fleet to confess themselves before going farther. In which he himself showed the way to the others. Moreover he would not allow any woman, whoever she might be, to come into the fleet and to the ships, for many good reasons.

* San Juan de Aznalfarache.
† San Lúcar de Barrameda, the port of departure for Spanish voyages to America.
‡ Cape St Vincent is over 100 miles from San Lúcar. The source of this error, evidently originating with Pigafetta or the scribe of the prototype, is un--known.

CHAPTER IV

Departure of the fleet from San Lucar. The captain, sailing continually, arrived at an island of the Grand Canary, where is no water but rain from heaven.

Tuesday the twentieth of September of the said year, we departed from San Lucar, laying course by the southwest wind, otherwise called *labeiche*. And on the sixteenth* of the said month we arrived at an island of the Grand Canary named Tenerife, in twenty-eight degrees of latitude,† where we remained three and a half days to take in provisions and other things which were needed. Then we departed thence and came to a port called Monterose,‡ where we remained two days to furnish ourselves with pitch, which is a thing very necessary for ships. Know that among the other islands which belong to the said Grand Canary, there is one where no drop of water coming from spring or river is found, save that once a day at the hour of noon there descends from heaven a cloud which encompasses a great tree in the said island, then all its leaves fall from it, and from the leaves is distilled great abundance of water, so that at the foot of the tree there is so great a quantity of water that it seems a living fountain. And from this water the inhabitants of the said place are satisfied, and the animals both domestic and wild.§

CHAPTER V

The captain and his fleet navigating in divers places and weather. Of the fish called Tiburoni. The body of St Anselm appeared to the ships. And of divers strange kinds and species of birds.

On Monday the third of October in the said year, at midnight, we sailed on the course to the south, which the seamen of the Levant call *cyroe*,|| [and] engulfing ourselves in the Ocean Sea, we passed

* The Italian Ms. dates the arrival at Tenerife 26 September; the Genoese pilot, 29 September.　　† In fact 28° 15′N.
‡ Punta Roxa, at the south end of Tenerife (Guillemard, p. 148).
§ This story about the island of Hierro goes back to Pliny.
|| *Cyroe* (*sirocco*), southeast wind.

Cape Verde and sailed for many [days] along the coast of Guinea or Ethiopia, where there is a mountain called Sierra Leone, which is in eight degrees of latitude, according to the art and science of cosmography and astrology.* And sometimes we had the wind contrary, at others fair, and rain without wind.† Thus we sailed for sixty days of rain to the equinoctial line. Which was a thing very strange and uncommon, in the opinion of the old people and of those who had sailed there several times before. Notwithstanding, before reaching that equinoctial line, we had in fourteen degrees a variety of weather, and bad, both by squalls and by wind and currents which came head-on to us so that we could not advance. And in order that our ships should not perish or broach to (as often happens when squalls come together), we struck the sails. And in this way we went up and down in the sea until good weather came.

During the calm great fish called *tiburoni* approached the ships.‡ They have terrible teeth and eat men when they find them alive or dead in the sea. And the said fish are caught with a hook of iron, with which some were taken by our people. But they are not good to eat when large. And even the small ones are not much good. During these storms the body of St Anslem appeared to us several times.§ And among others on a night which was very dark, at a time of bad weather, the said saint appeared in the form of a lighted torch at the height of the maintop, and remained there more than two hours and a half, to the comfort of us all. For we were in tears, expecting only the hour of death. And when this holy light was about to leave us, it was so bright to the eyes of all that we were for more than a

---

* Correct latitude, 8° 31′N.

† By following the African coast south and southeast, from the Canaries to Sierra Leone, taking 60 days to reach the equator, Magellan was delayed by the equatorial calms in the 'doldrums'. Why, drawing on the experience of Portuguese pilots since Cabral's voyage in 1499–1500, he did not take the *volta do mar largo*, southwest into the ocean from the Canaries, is not known and has been the subject of much speculation.

‡ *Tiburoni*, sharks.

§ St Elmo's fire, or corposant (*corpo santo*), electrical discharges seen at mastheads in stormy weather and taken to be a sign of divine protection.

quarter of an hour as blind men calling for mercy. For without any doubt no man thought he would escape from that storm. Be it noted that, whenever this fire which represents the said St Anslem appears and descends on a ship (which is in a storm at sea), the ship never perishes. Suddenly when the said fire vanished, the sea became calm again, and then we saw several birds of divers kinds. Among others there were some which had no rump. There is also another species of bird of such kind that, when the female wishes to lay its eggs, she goes to do so on the back of the male, and there they are hatched.★ And the birds of this last kind have no feet and are always in the sea. And there is another kind of bird which lives on nothing else but the ordure of other birds (this thing is true), and they are called *cagaselo*.† For I have seen it follow the other birds until they drop ordure. And after eating this ordure and dung, it no longer follows the other birds until hunger again comes upon it; and always it behaves in the same way. There are also flying fish, of which we saw so great a quantity together that it seemed an island in the sea.

CHAPTER VI

The captain and his fleet arrive at the land of Verzin. In what degrees it lies toward the Antarctic Pole. Of the desire of the people of that land to have goods from the captain. And of the Zenith.

After we had passed the equinoctial line toward the south, we lost the north star, and sailed between the south wind and *garbin*,‡ which is the wind between the said south and west, and we crossed to a land named Verzin,§ which is in twenty-four and a half degrees

★ The storm petrel. The legend was originally associated with the bird of paradise.

† The parasitic jaeger. The pursuit of gulls and terns by the jaeger was not (as popularly believed) to obtain their dung, but to make them disgorge fish they had swallowed.

‡ *Garbin*, synonymous with *laberche*, southwest wind.

§ Brazil, from the Italian *verzino*, brazil-wood, which gave the name to the country first called Vera Cruz by its discoverer Cabral, and subsequently Santa Cruz. The modern name was already in use in Magellan's time.

toward the Antarctic Pole.★ Which land extends from Cape St Augustine, which is in eight degrees toward the said Antarctic Pole. In which place we replenished our provisions, as with fowl and calves' flesh, also a variety of fruits named *battate*,† and sweet pineapples of singular goodness, and infinite other things which I pass over that I be not too long. The people of this place gave for a knife or a fishhook five or six fowls, and for a comb a brace of geese. For a small mirror or a pair of scissors, they gave as many fish as ten men could have eaten. For a bell or a leather lace, they gave a basketful of the said fruit called *battate*. Which tastes like a chestnut, and is of the length of a turnip. And for a king of playing cards, of the kind used in Italy, they gave me five fowls, and even thought they had cheated me. We entered the said port on the day of Santa Lucia, at the advent of Christmas, on which day we had the sun at the zenith, which is a term of astrology. This zenith is a point in the heavens which (according to astrologers, and only in the imagination) lies in a direct line above our head. As may be seen in the *Treatise of the Sphere* and in Aristotle's first book *De celo et mundo*.‡ And the day that we had the sun in the zenith, we felt the heat greater than when we were on the equinoctial line.

★ The sense, here corrupt, is presumably: 'Verzin extends southward to $24\frac{1}{2}°$S,' or, 'Verzin extends $24\frac{1}{2}$ degrees southward toward the Pole.' Land was sighted near Pernambuco (in 8°S) on 29 November; after coasting southwest past Cape Frio, they entered the harbour of Rio de Janeiro (a name already in use), on St Lucia's day, 13 December, calling it after the saint.

† *Battate*, sweet potatoes.

‡ The *Treatise of the Sphere* is doubtless Pigafetta's treatise.

CHAPTER VII

The fleet arrives at the land of Verzin. The opulence of that land. The manner of the inhabitants' living and sleeping. Of their boats. The people eat the flesh of their enemies. Their accoutrements. The making of their bread. Of the honest dealing of the said inhabitants of Verzin toward the captain and his men. And of the very great simplicity of those people.

The said land of Verzin abounds in all good things, and it is larger than France, Spain and Italy together. It is one of the countries that the King of Portugal has conquered. Its people are not Christians, and worship nothing, but live according to the custom of nature, more like beasts than otherwise.★ And some of these people live a hundred years, or six score or seven score years, or more, and they go naked, both men and women. Their habitation is in fairly long houses, which they call *boii*, and they sleep in nets of cotton, which they call in their language *amache*.† Which nets are fastened to great beams from one end of their house to the other. And to warm them they make a fire on the ground immediately below their bed. And know that in each of these houses called *boii* there lives a family of one hundred persons, who make much noise. And in this place there are boats, made from a tree all in one piece, which they call *canoe*.‡ They are not made with tools of iron (for they have none), but with stones like pebbles with which they plane and hollow the said boats. These boats hold thirty or forty men. And their paddles are made like iron shovels. And those who wield the paddles are black men all naked and shaved, and they look like enemies from hell.

The men and women of this place are of good physical build. They eat the flesh of their enemies, not as being good for food, but from custom. The origin of this custom is as follows. An old woman of this land of Verzin had an only son who was killed by his enemies, and some days later the friends of this woman took one of the said

★ The people described were a tribe of the Tupi or Guarani Indians.

† Hammocks; the word was introduced into European languages by the records of this voyage.

‡ Another word brought back to Europe by Magellan's men.

enemies who had caused her son's death, and brought him to the
place where she was. She, seeing the man who was taken and re-
membering her son's death, ran incontinent upon him like an angry
bitch and bit him in his shoulder. But he managed to run away and
escape. And he told how they had tried to eat him, showing the bite
which that woman had made in his shoulder. After that, those who
were captured on one side or the other were eaten. Whence came
the custom in this country of eating one another's enemies. They do
not eat the whole body of the man taken, but eat it piece by piece.
For fear that he be not tasted, they cut him up in pieces which they
put to dry in the chimney, and every day they cut off a small piece
and eat it with their ordinary food to call to mind their enemies. I
was assured that this custom was true by a pilot named João Carvalho, who was in our company and had lived four years in that
country.*

Be it noted also that the inhabitants of that country, both men
and women, are in the habit of painting themselves with fire over
all the body and face.† The men are shaved and wear no beard, for
they pluck it out themselves. And their whole clothing is a ring
surrounded by the largest parrot feathers, with which they cover
the part and backside only. Which is a very ridiculous thing. Almost
all the men of this place (but not the women and children) have
three holes in the lower lip and wear small round stones about a
finger in length hanging from them. And those people, both men
and women, are not quite black, but tend to tan colour, and they
openly display their shame, and have no hair on any part of their
person.

The king of this place is called *Carich*.‡ And there are great

---

* João Lopes Carvalho, pilot of *Concepción*, is known to have piloted the Portu-
guese ship *Bretoa* to Brazil in 1511. His four years' residence there seems to be
unrecorded except by Pigafetta, who refers later to Carvalho's son, by a
Brazilian woman, who was serving in the fleet and was made prisoner in
Borneo.
† This is Pigafetta's regular formula for describing tattooing.
‡ *Cacich*, i.e. cacique.

numbers of parrots there, of which they give eight or ten for a mirror. There are also pretty little cats very like a lion, yellow and beautiful in appearance.* These people make bread in round loaves and take the marrow from certain trees of the place, between the bark and the wood. But this is not very good, being like fresh cheese.† There are also swine which have their navel on their back,‡ and large birds with spoon-shaped beak and no tongue.§ For a hatchet or for a knife they gave us one or two of their daughters for slaves. But they would not give their wives for anything at all. The women also would not on any account shame their husbands. As we were told, the women of this place never pay service to their husbands by day, but only by night. They attend to affairs outside, and carry everything that they need for their husbands' food in little baskets on their head or fastened to their head. Their husbands go with them and carry a bow of brazil or of black palm wood with a bundle of cane arrows, and they do this because they are very jealous of their wives. The women carry their children bound to their neck in a thing made of cotton in the fashion of a net.

I omit to relate many other strange things, that I be not too prolix. But I would not forget to say that mass was twice said on land, at which were many people of the said country, kneeling with folded hands in great reverence during the mass, that it was a pleasure and compassion to see them. And in a short time they built a house for us, thinking that we were to abide a long time with them, and at our departure they gave us a great quantity of *verzin*. This is a colour which comes from trees which are in the said place, in so great a quantity that its country is called Verzin. Know that it chanced that there had been no rain for two months before we came thither, and the day when we arrived the rain began, so that the people of the place said that we came from heaven and had brought the rain with us. Which was a great simplicity. And certainly these

* Presumably monkeys of the genus *Cebus*.
† This was perhaps manioc or cassava, from the root of which bread is made in Brazil.
‡ Apparently the peccary or 'wart hog'.   § The roseate spoonbill.

people would be easily converted to the Christian faith. Besides the above-mentioned things (betraying their simplicity) the people of this place showed us another very simple thing. For they thought that the small boats of the ships were the children of the ships, and that the said ships gave birth to them when the boats were lowered to send the men hither and yon. And when the boats were lying alongside a ship, they thought that the ships were suckling them. A beautiful young girl came one day on board our captain's ship, in which I was, and for no purpose than to seek her fortune. Meanwhile she raised her eyes toward the master's cabin, where she saw a nail of a finger's length, which she took and merrily hid it, as something great and new, within her nature, and straightway ran off bending forward. And the captain and I saw this mystery.

Some Words of the Peoples of Verzin

Millett *Maiz*	A comb *Chiguap*
Flour *Huy*	Scissors *Pirame*
A fishhook *Pinda*	A bell *Iteumaraca*
A knife *Taisse*	Good, better *Tum, maragatum*

CHAPTER VIII

The captain, arriving near a river, found the men called Canibali, one of whom came to the ship. Of the islands of this river. Other islands where the captain came. Of another port where he came. Of some giants whom he found there. The manner in which he held two of them in his ships. Of the two whom he dismissed. And of the devils who attend at the death of those giants.

We tarried thirteen days in this land of Verzin, and departing thence and pursuing our way we went to thirty-four and one third degrees toward the Antarctic Pole. There we found beside a river men of the kind called *canibali*, who eat human flesh.★ And one of these men, as tall as a giant, came to our captain's ship to satisfy himself and request that the others might come. And this

★ *Canibali*, a transfer word from Caribs, to whom Columbus on his first voyage attributed the practice of man-eating.

man had a voice like a bull's. And while he was on board the ship, his companions carried off all their goods which they had to a more distant castle, for fear of us. Seeing this, we landed one hundred men from the ships and went after them to try to take some. But they made their escape, for these people made more ground in one pace than we could in a leap.

In the said river were seven small islands, in the largest of which precious stones are found. Which place was formerly named Cape St Mary, and it was thought that one passed thence to the sea of Sur★ and nothing more was ever discovered. It is not known that any ships have passed beyond the said cape. And now it is no longer a cape, but a river, seventeen leagues in width at its mouth, where it enters the sea.† In time past these tall men called *canibali*, in this river, ate a Spanish captain named Juan de Solis and sixty men who had gone, as we did, to discover land, trusting too much in them.‡ Then following the same course toward the Antarctic Pole, coasting along the land,§ we discovered two islands full of geese and goslings and sea wolves. The great number of these goslings‖ there were cannot be estimated, for we loaded all the ships with them in an hour. And these goslings are black and have feathers over their whole body of the same size and fashion, and they do not fly, and they live on fish. And they were so fat that we did not pluck them but skinned them, and they have a beak like a crow's. The sea wolves¶ of these

★ The South Sea.
† This means that the name Santa Maria had been transferred from the cape (still so called), on which it had been bestowed by Juan de Solis in 1515, to the estuary of the Rio de la Plata.
‡ Juan Diaz de Solis, pilot-major of Spain, had sailed in October 1515 for the discovery of a passage to the Indies by the southwest, that is, with the same objective as Magellan; he and some of his men were killed and eaten in 1516 by La Plata Indians.
§ Pigafetta simplifies the course of events. Magellan had spent two days sailing up the estuary and six days at anchor in it, before resuming his voyage southward on 3 February 1520.
‖ Penguins.
¶ Fur seals.

two islands are of various colours and of the size and thickness of a calf, and they have a head like that of a calf, and small round ears. They have large teeth and no legs, but they have feet attached to their body and resembling a human hand. And they have feet, nails on their feet, and skin between the toes like goslings. And if these animals could run, they would be very fierce and cruel. But they do not leave the water, where they swim and live on fish.

In this place we ran very great risk of perishing. But the three bodies of St Anselm, St Nicholas, and St Clare appeared to us, and forthwith the storm ceased. Departing thence to forty-nine and a half degrees toward the Antarctic Pole, because it was winter, we entered a port to pass the winter,* where we remained two whole months without ever seeing anyone. But one day (without anyone expecting it) we saw a giant who was on the shore, quite naked, and who danced, leaped, and sang, and while he sang he threw sand and dust on his head. Our captain sent one of his men toward him, charging him to leap and sing like the other in order to reassure him and show him friendship. Which he did. Immediately the man of the ship, dancing, led this giant to a small island where the captain awaited him. And when he was before us, he began to marvel and to be afraid, and he raised one finger upward, believing that we came from heaven. And he was so tall that the tallest of us only came up to his waist. Withal he was well proportioned.† He had a very large face, painted round with red, and his eyes also were painted round with yellow, and in the middle of his cheeks he had two hearts painted. He had hardly any hairs on his head, and they were painted white. When he was brought to the captain, he was clad in the skin of a certain animal, which skin was very skillfully sewn together. And this animal has the head and ears as large as a mule's, and a neck and body like those of a camel, a stag's legs, and a tail like that of a

* Puerto San Julián, reached on 31 March 1520.
† The belief in the great stature of the Patagonian 'giants', which was to have a long life, begins with the reports by Magellan's expedition of the Tehuelche Indians encountered.

horse.★ And there are great numbers of these animals in the said place. This giant had his feet covered with the skin of the said animal in the manner of shoes, and he carried in his hand a short thick bow, with a thick bowstring, made from the intestines of the said animal, with a bundle of cane arrows which were not very long and were feathered like ours, but had no iron point but, at the tip, small black and white stones cut to a sharp point. And they were like the arrows used by the Turks.

The captain caused the giant to be given food and drink, then he showed him other things, among them a steel mirror. Wherein the giant seeing himself was greatly terrified, leaping back so that he threw four of our men to the ground. After that the captain gave him two bells, a mirror, a comb, and a chaplet of paternosters, and sent him back on shore, causing him to be accompanied by four armed men. One of the giant's companions, who would never come to the ship, seeing the other return with our men, advanced and ran before to the place where the other giants lived. And they placed themselves one after the other quite naked and began to leap and sing, raising one finger to the sky, and showing our people a certain white powder made from roots of herbs, which they kept in earthenware pots, and made signs that they lived on that, and that they had nothing else to eat but this powder. Whereupon our men made signs to them that they should come to the ships, and that they would help them to carry their provisions. Then these men came, bearing only their bows in their hands. But their wives came after them loaded like asses and carrying their goods. And the women are not so tall as the men, but somewhat fatter. When we saw them, we were all amazed and astonished. For they had teats half a cubit long, and they were painted on the face and clad like the men. But they wore a small skin in front to cover their private parts. They brought with them four of those little animals of which they make their clothing, and led them on a leash with a cord. When these people wish to catch these animals by whom they are clothed, they tie one of the young ones to a bush, and thereupon the large ones

★ The guanaco, related to the llama.

come to play with the little ones, and the giants hidden behind some ledge kill with their arrows the large ones.

Our men took eighteen of these giants, both men and women, whom they divided into two parties, half on one side of the port and the other half on the other, to catch the said animals. Six days later, our men going to cut wood saw another giant, painted on the face and clad like the others, who had in his hand a bow and arrows, and approaching our men he touched his head several times, and afterward his body, then he did the same to our men. This done, he raised his two hands to heaven. The captain-general, learning this, sent to fetch him in his ship's boat, and took him to one of the small islands in the port where his ships lay. On this island the captain had caused a house to be built to store some things of his ships while he remained there. This giant was of better disposition than the others, and was very graceful and amiable, loving to dance and leap. And when dancing he depressed the earth to a palm's depth in the spot where his feet touched. He was with us for a long time, and in the end we baptized him, naming him John. The said giant pronounced the name Jesus, the Pater Noster, Ave Maria, and his own name as clearly as we. But he had a terribly loud and strong voice. The captain gave him a shirt and a cloth jerkin, and seaman's breeches, a cap, a mirror, a comb, bells and other things, and sent him away whence he had come; and he went off very joyous and happy. The next day the said giant returned and brought some of those large animals aforesaid, for which the captain gave him other things, that he might bring more. But he did not return again. And it is to be supposed that the other giants killed him because he had come to us.

Fifteen days later we saw four other giants who were not carrying weapons (for they had hidden them in the bushes, as two of them showed us). For we took them all four, and each pair of them was painted in a different manner. The captain kept the two youngest to bring them to Spain on his return. But this was by a cunning trick, for otherwise they would have troubled some of our men. The means by which he kept them was that he gave them many knives, scissors, mirrors, bells and glass, all which things they held in their hands. And meanwhile the captain sent for large iron fetters, such as are put on the feet of malefactors. Whereat these giants took great pleasure in seeing these fetters, and did not know where they had to be put, and they were grieved that they could not take them in their hands, because they were prevented by the other things aforesaid. The two giants who were there wished to help these two. But the captain refused, and made signs to the two whom he wished to keep that the fetters would be put on their feet, [and] then they would go away. Whereat they made a sign with their heads that they were content with this. Forthwith the captain had the fetters put on the feet of both of them. And when they saw the bolt across the fetters being struck with a hammer to rivit it and prevent them from being opened, these giants were afraid. But the captain made signs to them that they should suspect nothing. Nevertheless, perceiving the trick that had been played on them, they began to blow and foam at the mouth like bulls, loudly calling on *Setebos*** (that is, the great devil) to help them. And the hands of the other two were tied, but with great difficulty.

Then the captain sent them ashore with nine of his men to escort them and to fetch the wife of one of the two men who were kept in fetters, because he was greatly lamenting her (as we saw by his gestures). But, as they went away, one of the two who were sent back untied his hands and escaped, running with so much nimbleness that our men lost sight of him, and he went off to the place where his companions had been. But he did not find any of those whom he had left with the women, because they had gone hunting. Whereupon he at once went in search of them, found them and related all that had been done to them. The other giant who had his hands bound made the utmost efforts to free himself, so that to prevent him one of our men struck him and wounded his head, at which he was violently angry. But our men took him to the place where

* A Tehuelche word, borrowed by Shakespeare (*The Tempest*, I.ii and V.i) from Richard Eden's translation of Pigafetta in *The Decades of the newe worlde* (1555).

their wives were. Then João Carvalho the pilot (who commanded the escort of these two giants) refused to bring away the wife of one of the two giants in fetters that evening, but decided to sleep there, since it was almost night. And meantime the giant who had unbound his hands returned whence he had gone with another giant, who seeing their companion wounded in the head said nothing at that time. But the next morning they spoke in their language to the women, and forthwith all fled together (the smaller ones ran faster than the taller ones) and left behind all their possessions.

Then two of these giants, at a certain distance, shot arrows at our men, and fighting thus, one of these giants pierced one of our men in the thigh, who died immediately. Whereupon seeing him dead they all fled away. Our men had crossbows and muskets, but they could never hit any of those people because they never stood in one place, but leaped hither and thither. This done, our men buried the dead man and made a fire in the place where those giants had left their possessions. And verily those giants run straighter than a horse, and are very jealous of their wives. When these giants have pain in the stomach, instead of taking medicine, they put down their throat an arrow two feet or thereabout in length, then they vomit of a green colour mingled with blood. And the reason why they bring up this green matter is that they often eat thistles. And when they have a headache, they make a cut across their forehead, and the same on the arms and legs, to draw blood from several parts of their body. One of the two kept in our ship said that the blood refused to stop at the place and part of the body where the pain was felt. These people have the hair cut short and shaved like friars, with the tonsure. And they wear a cotton cord round their head, to which they fasten their arrows when they go hunting, and bind their member close to the body by reason of the very great cold. When one of them dies, ten or twelve devils appear, and dance round the dead man. And it seems they are painted. And one of these devils is taller than the others, and makes much more noise, and rejoices much more than the others. And from this the giants took the fashion of painting themselves on the face and body, as has been said. And in their language they called the largest of these devils *Setebos*, and the others *Cheleule*. Besides the things aforesaid, he who was in the ship told us by signs that he had seen devils with two horns on their head, and with long hair down to their feet, and through their mouth and backside they belched fire.

The captain named the people of this sort *Pathagoni*.* They have no houses. But they have boats made of the skin of the aforesaid animals from which they clothe themselves. And they go hither and thither in the said boats, as the Egyptians do. They live on raw flesh, and eat a certain sweet root which they call *Capae*. Those two giants whom we had in the ship ate a large boxful of biscuit, and un-skinned rats, and they drank half a pailful of water at a time.

CHAPTER IX

Of the treachery plotted against the captain. Punishment and names of the traitors. Of a ship lost, and the men saved. Of Port St Julian. And of a river to which the captain came.

We remained in this port (which was called Port St Julian) about five months,† where many strange things befell us. One was that, as soon as we entered the port, the masters of the other four ships conspired against the captain-general to bring about his death. Whose names were Juan de Cartagena, overseer of the fleet, the treasurer Luis de Mendoza, the overseer Antonio de Coca, and Gaspar Quesada.‡ But the treachery was discovered, because the

---

* The name bestowed by Magellan exists, with the sense of 'dogs with large paws', in various romance languages: Spanish *patacones*, Portuguese *patas de cão*, French *patauds*.

† From 31 March to 24 August 1520.

‡ Juan de Cartagena, *veedor general* of the fleet, had been captain of the *S. Antonio* on sailing, but before crossing the Equator had been court-martialled and deprived of his command, which was given to Antonio de Coca, *contador* of the fleet. At Port St Julian the latter was replaced by Alvaro de Mesquita, a Portuguese and Magellan's cousin (or nephew). This seems to have sparked

treasurer was killed by dagger blows, then quartered. This Gaspar
Quesada had his head cut off, and then he was quartered. And the
overseer Juan de Cartagena, who several days later tried to commit
treachery, was banished with a priest, and put in exile on that land
named *Patagoni*. The captain-general did not wish to put to death
this overseer, because the Emperor Charles had made him captain
of one of the ships. And one of the ships called Santiago going to discover the coast was lost.* But all the men were saved by a miracle,
for they were not even wetted. Two of the men who were saved
came to us and told us all that had happened and had been done.
Whereupon the captain forthwith sent some men with sacks full of
biscuit for two months' supply to the others who had escaped from
the ship that was lost. So that every day we found something from
the ship. And the place where those men were was twenty-five
leagues distant from us, and the road bad and full of thorns, and it
took four days to go thither, and there was no water to drink on the
road, except from ice, and little enough of that. In this Port St
Julian there were a great number of long shellfish called *missiglioni*,†
which had pearls in the middle. And in this place are found incense,
ostriches, foxes, sparrows and coneys somewhat smaller than ours.
On the top of the highest mountain there we set up a very tall cross,
as a sign that the said land belonged to the King of Spain. And we
gave this mountain the name Mont de Christ.

Departing thence,‡ in fifty-one degrees less a third of a degree

* João Serrão had been appointed captain of *Santiago* after the mutiny. She had
coasted southward to Puerto Santa Cruz and was wrecked three leagues beyond it on 22 May. One man only, of the crew of 37, was lost.

† Spanish *mejillón*, an edible shellfish, perhaps the mussel.

‡ On 24 August, leaving behind Juan de Cartagena and another mutineer.
The ships' captains were now all Portuguese, and relatives or close friends of
Magellan.

---

off the conspiracy on the night of 1–2 April, when the mutineers, led by Juan
de Cartagena, Juan Sebastian de Elcano, Gaspar Quesada (captain of *Concepción*) and Luis de Mendoza (captain of *Victoria* and treasurer of the fleet),
made themselves masters of the three largest ships.

le capitaine voulut que tous se confessassent, et receussent le corps
de nostre seigneur, comme bons crestiens.

Le Capitaine arriua a vng Cap. quil nomma Le Cap des onze
mille vierges. Puys vint au Cap de la Baya. Deux naures enuoy
pour trouuer la saillie dudit Cap. Dune bouche quelles trouue
pour sortir du cap. En la quelle se gecterent a force. Puys ayan
de scouuert le destroict sen retournerent vers le capitaine.

Chapitre. x.

Pres allant, et prenant la voye au cinquante, et
deuxiesme degre audit ciel antarticque, le iour
de la feste des onze mille vierges, nous trouuas
mes par miracle vng estroict que nous appellasmes le Cap
de onze mille vierges. Le quel estroict a de longueur, cent et
dix lieues, qui sont quatre cents et quarante mille, et quasi
autant de largeur, moins de demye lieue. Et va tumber en
vne aultre mer, quon appelle La mer paisible. Et est enuiro
nee de fort grandes et haultes montaignes chargees de neige.

En cedit lieu ne fut possible de surgir auecq les anctres
Pource quon ne trouuoit point de fondz. Par quoy fut force
de meetre les proisses en terre, de vingt et cinq ou trente
brasses de longueur. Le quel estroict estoit vng lieu rond
enuironne de montaignes (comme iay dit) Et a la plus gra
partie des naures sembloit quil ny eust point de lieu pou
saillir de la, pour entrer en ladicte mer paisible. Mais le
capitaine general dist quil y auoit vng aultre estroit po
saillir, disant quil le scauoit bien, et lauoit veu par vne

Le capitaine tirant a
la mer paisible arriua
au cap des onze mille
vierges.

Du cap des onze
mille vierges.

toward the Antarctic, we found a river of fresh water,* which almost caused us to perish for the great winds which it gave forth. But God by his grace succoured us. We were about two months in this river, to supply ourselves with water, wood, and a kind of fish a cubit long and very scaly, and good to eat. Before departing thence† the captain desired all to confess themselves and to receive the body of our Lord, as good Christians.

CHAPTER X

The captain came to a cape, which he named the Cape of the Eleven Thousand Virgins. Then he came to the Cape de la Baya. Two ships sent to find the way out from the said cape. Of an opening which they found for leaving the cape, and into which they threw themselves perforce. Then having discovered the strait they returned to the captain.

After going and setting course to the fifty-second degree toward the said Antarctic Pole, on the festival of the eleven thousand virgins, we found by miracle a strait which we called the Cape of the Eleven Thousand Virgins.‡ Which strait is in length one hundred and ten leagues, which are four hundred and forty miles, and in width somewhat less than half a league. And it falls into another sea called the Pacific Sea. And it is surrounded by very great and high mountains covered with snow. In this place it was not possible to anchor, because no bottom was found. Wherefore it was necessary to put cables ashore of twenty-five or thirty cubits in length. This strait was a circular place surrounded by mountains (as I have said), and to most of those in the ships it seemed that there was no way out from it to enter the said Pacific Sea. But the captain-general said that there was another strait which led out, saying that he knew it

* The Puerto Santa Cruz, discovered by Serrão in *Santiago* on 3 May, the festival of the Invention of the Cross.
† On 18 October.
‡ Cabo Virjenes, marking the eastern end of the Strait of Magellan, discovered on 21 October 1520.

well and had seen it in a marine chart of the King of Portugal, which a great pilot and sailor named Martin of Bohemia had made. The said captain sent forward two of his ships, one named Santo Antonio and the other Concepción, to seek and discover the outlet of the said strait, which was called the Cape de la Baya.* And we with the other two ships (namely the *capitana*, named Trinidade, and the other Victoria) remained awaiting them in the Baya. And in the night we had a great storm, which lasted until noon of the next day. Wherefore we were compelled to raise the anchors, and to let the ships ply hither and thither in the Baya.

The other two ships had such a passage that they could not round a cape forming the Baya,† and trying to return to us they were hard put not to run aground. But approaching the end of the Baya (thinking themselves lost) they saw a small opening, which did not seem an opening but a creek.‡ And like desperate men they threw themselves into it, so that perforce they discovered the strait. Then seeing that it was not a creek but a strait with land, they went on, and found a bay.§ Then going further they found another strait, and another bay larger than the first two.|| Very joyful at this, they at once turned back to inform the captain-general. We thought indeed that they had perished, first because of the great storm, and then we had not seen them for two days. And while in suspense we saw the two ships approaching under full sail and flying their banners, coming toward us. When near us, they suddenly discharged their ordnance, at which we very joyously greeted them in the same way. And then we all together, thanking God and the Virgin Mary, went forward.

* Lomas Bay, on the south shore of the Strait; or (less probably) Possession Bay, on the north shore.
† Probably Punta Anegada.
‡ *Canton.* The First Narrows, west of Punta Anegada.
§ Bahía S. Felipe.
|| The Second Narrows and Broad Reach.

CHAPTER XI

Two ships, the Santo Antonio and Concepción, sent to see the two openings found. The ship Santo Antonio returned to Spain. The river of the Sardines found. The sea found. Of the Cape of Desire. Of the ship Concepción. Of the products of this Pacific Sea. And of the catching of fish.

After entering within this strait, we found that there were two openings, one of them to the southeast, and the other to the southwest.* Wherefore the captain sent back the two aforesaid ships Santo Antonio and Concepción to see whether the opening toward the southeast issued forth into the said Pacific Sea. And the one of these two ships named Santo Antonio would not await the other ship, because those on board her wished to return to Spain, which they did. And the principal reason was that the pilot of the said ship had before been displeased with the said captain-general,† because, before this fleet was fitted out, this pilot had gone to the Emperor to arrange to have some ships for discovering land. But by the coming of the said captain-general the Emperor did not give them to the said pilot. Wherefore he conspired with certain Spaniards. And the following night they seized the captain of his ship, who was the captain-general's brother, and named Alvaro de Mesquita, whom they wounded and put in irons. And so they took it back to Spain.‡

In this ship which went away was one of the aforesaid two giants whom we had taken, but when he felt the heat he died. And the

* Presumably Admiralty Sound and Magdalen Sound. Other accounts show that, while *S. Antonio* and *Concepción* reconnoitred the former channel, *Trinidad* and *Victoria* proceeded up Froward Reach, the main channel.

† Estevão Gomes, a Portuguese relative of Magellan, had himself formulated a plan for an expedition of discovery, which was forestalled by Magellan's.

‡ *Santo Antonio* reached Seville on 6 May 1521. The mutineers were acquitted, and Mesquita, her captain, remained in prison until the return of *Victoria* in September 1522. Gomes was to lead an important expedition of discovery along the Atlantic coasts of North America in 1524–25.

other ship Concepción (because she could not keep up with the former) continued to wait for her, plying hither and thither. For the other took the night course (as they say) in order to return. When this happened by night, the captain's ship and the other ship went together to discover the other opening to the southwest, and continuing on we found the same strait. But at length we came to a river which we called the River of Sardines, because we found great quantity of them. And so we remained there four days awaiting the other two ships.

Soon after we sent a boat well furnished with men and provisions to discover the cape of the other sea. They spent three days going and returning, and told us that they had found the cape and the great and wide sea. Wherefore the captain, for the joy that he had, began to weep and gave this cape the name Cape of Desire, as a thing much desired and long sought. This done, we turned back to find the two ships which had gone to the other side, but we found only Concepción, of whom we demanded what had become of the other, her consort. To which the captain of the said ship, named João Serrão (who was pilot of the first ship that was lost, as has been told), replied that he knew nothing and that he had never seen her since she entered the opening. But we sought for her throughout the strait as far as the said opening by which she set her course for return. And besides this, the captain-general sent back the ship named Victoria to the very entrance of the strait to see whether the said ship was not there. And he told the men of this ship, if they did not find the other ship that was missing, to put a flag on the summit of a small mountain, with a letter in a pot buried at the foot of the staff, to the end that if the said ship perchance returned she would see this flag and also find the letter, which would inform her of the course taken by the captain.* This arrangement had from the beginning been ordered by the captain, to cause any ship which was separated to rejoin the others. So the people of the said ship did what the captain had ordered, and more. For they set up two flags

* All three remaining ships searched Admiralty Sound, and the *Victoria* returned to the eastern entrance of the Strait.

with letters. One of the flags was set up on a small mountain at the first bay, the second on an islet in the third bay, where there were many sea wolves and large birds.* The captain-general waited for her with the other ship near the river named Isleo.† And he caused a cross to be erected on a small island near that river. The river flowed between high mountains covered with snow, and it fell into the sea near the other River of Sardines.

If we had not found this strait, the captain-general had decided to go as far as seventy-five degrees toward the Antarctic Pole. Now in such a latitude, in the summertime, there is no night, or very little. And likewise in winter there is no day, or very little. And that all may believe that this is so, when we were in the said strait, the night lasted only three hours in the month of October.

The land on the left in the said strait faced toward the *siroco*, which is the wind between east and south. And we called it the Pathagonico strait.‡ In it we found at every half league a good port, and anchorage, good water, and wood all of cedar, and fish also like sardines, *missiglioni*, and a very sweet herb called *appio*, of which there is also some of the same sort that is bitter.§ And this herb grows near springs, and (because we found nothing else) we ate of it for several days. And I think there is in the world no more beautiful country or better place than that.

In that Ocean Sea there is seen a very amusing hunt of fishes, which are of three sorts, a cubit or more in length, named *dorades*, *albacores*, and *boniti*. They follow and hunt another kind of fish which flies and is called *colondriny*, a foot or more in length and very good to eat.|| And when these three kinds of fish find in the water some of these flying fish, forthwith they make them leave the water and

* The 'first bay' was Lomas Bay or Possession Bay; the 'islet in the third bay', perhaps Santa Magdalena Island (Isla de los Patos) in Broad Reach.
† The River of Isles.
‡ According to the Genoese pilot, the strait was named 'the Strait of Victoria, because the ship *Victoria* was the first that had seen it; some called it the Strait of Magalhãens because our captain was named Fernando de Magalhãens.'
§ A wild celery recommended by later navigators as an antiscorbutic.
|| Spanish *golondrina* = gurnard.

fly more than a crossbow's flight as long as their wings are wet. And while these fish fly, the other three run after them in the water seeing and following the shadow of those that fly. And no sooner have they fallen than they are seized and eaten by those which hunt them. Which is a marvellous and merry thing to see. And this chase we saw several times.

*Words of the Pathagonian Giants**

The head *Her*
The eyes *Other*
The nose *Or*
The eyelids *Occhechel*
The eyelashes *Sechechiel*
The nostrils *Oresche*
The mouth *Xiam*
The lips *Schiame*
The teeth *Phor*
The tongue *Schial*
The chin *Sechen*
The hair *Aschir*
The face *Cogechel*
The throat *Ohumér*
The stomach *Schialeschin*
The shoulders *Peles*
The elbow *Cotel*
The hand *Chene*
The palm *Caimeghin*
The finger *Cori*
The arm *Mar*
The ears *Sane*
The armpits *Salischin*
The teat *Othen*
The breast *Ochii*
The thumb *Ochon*

The body *Gechel*
The penis *Scachet*
The testicles *Sacaneos*
The vagina *Isse*
Intercourse with women *Iohoi*
The thighs *Chiaue*
The knee *Tepin*
The rump *Schiachen*
The buttocks *Hoii*
The legs *Choss*
The feet *Tehe*
The heel *There*
The ankle *Perchi*
The sole of the foot *Coatscheni*
The nails *Colim*
The heart *Thol*
To scratch *Ghecare*
The old man *Calischen*
The young [man] *Callemi*
Water *Oli*
Fire *Ghialeme*
We *Ehen*
Smoke *Iaiche*
Yes *Rei*
Gold *Pelpeli*
Precious stone *Secheghi*

* The earliest recorded vocabulary of the Tehuelche of Patagonia.

The sun *Calex cheni*

The stars *Settere*

The sea *Aro*

The wind *Oni*

The storm *Ohone*

Fish *Hoi*

To eat *Mecchiere*

A bowl *Elo*

A basket *Aschaine*

To ask *Ghelhe*

Come here *Haisi*

To look *Conne*

To go *Rhei*

To fight *Oamaghce*

Arrows *Sethe*

A dog *Holl*

A wolf *Ani*

To go far *Schien*

The guide *Anti*

The ship *Theu*

To run *Hiam*

Dead bird *Hoihoi*

Its eggs *Ian*

The powder of the herb which they eat *Capae*

To smell *Os*

Parrot *Cheche*

Birdcage *Cleo*

Missiglioni fish *Siameni*

Red cloth *Terechai*

The cap *Aichel*

Black colour *Amel*

Red *Theiche*

Yellow *Peperi*

To cook *Irecoles*

The belt *Cathechin*

A goose *Chache*

The great devil *Setebos*

Small devils *Cheleule*

These words were spoken to me by that giant whom we had in the ship. For when he, asking me for *capac*, that is bread (for so they call the root which they use for bread), and *oli*, that is water, saw me write down these names and afterward when I asked him for others, pen in hand, he understood me. Another time I made the sign of the cross, and kissed the cross, showing it to him. But at once he cried out *Setebos*, and he made signs to me that, if I made the sign of the cross again, it would enter my stomach and cause me to burst. When this giant was sick, he asked for the cross, and embraced and kissed it often. And he wished to become a Christian before his death. And we named him Paul.

When those people wish to make a fire, they take a pointed stick which they rub against another, until they cause fire to catch between these two sticks in the pith of a tree which is like cotton.

CHAPTER XII

*The captain in the Pacific Sea. The troubles which he and his men suffered
there. Of the malady in their gums. Of the dead and the sick men. Of the Isles
of Misfortune, and in what degree they lie.*

On Wednesday the twenty-eighth of November, one thousand
five hundred and twenty, we issued forth from the said strait*
and entered the Pacific Sea, where we remained three months and
twenty days without taking on board provisions or any other re-
freshments, and we ate only old biscuit turned to powder, all full of
worms and stinking of the urine which the rats had made on it,
having eaten the good. And we drank water impure and yellow.
We ate also ox hides which were very hard because of the sun, rain
and wind. And we left them four or five days in the sea, then laid
them for a short time on embers, and so we ate them. And of the
rats, which were sold for half an écu apiece, some of us could not get
enough. Besides the aforesaid troubles, this malady was the worst,
namely that the gums of most part of our men swelled above and
below so that they could not eat.† And in this way they died, inasmuch as twenty-nine of us died, and the other giant died, and an
Indian of the said country of Verzin. But besides those who died,
twenty-five or thirty fell sick of divers maladies, whether of the
arms or of the legs and other parts of the body, so that there remained very few healthy men. Yet by the grace of our Lord I had
no illness.

During these three months and twenty days, we sailed in a gulf
where we made a good four thousand leagues across the Pacific Sea,
which was rightly so named. For during this time we had no storm,
and we saw no land except two small uninhabited islands, where we
found only birds and trees. Wherefore we called them the Isles of
Misfortune.‡ And they are two hundred leagues distant one from

* The passage of the strait had lasted about 38 days.
† This was scurvy. The official list of deaths recorded only seven between the
Strait and the Ladrones.
‡ The first island was discovered after forty days' sailing on St Paul's day,

another. And there is no place for anchoring because no bottom can be found. And we saw there a very large kind of fish which they call *tiburoni.* The first island is in fifteen degrees of latitude going by the south wind, and the other island is in nine degrees. By this wind we made each day fifty or sixty leagues or more, sometimes at the stern, at others at the windward side, or otherwise. And if our Lord and the Virgin Mother had not aided us by giving good weather to refresh ourselves with provisions and other things we had died in this very great sea. And I believe that nevermore will any man undertake to make such a voyage.

CHAPTER XIII

Of the captain's fortune. Of the Antarctic Pole, what it is. Of the points of the chart corrected and restored to true. And the vision of stars that the captain had.

When we had left that strait, if we had sailed always westward, we should have gone without finding any island★ other than the Cape of the Eleven Thousand Virgins, which is the cape of that strait at the Ocean Sea, lying east–west with the Cape of Desire of the Pacific Sea. Which two capes are in fifty-two degrees of latitude exactly toward the Antarctic Pole. The Antarctic Pole is not so marked by stars as the Arctic. For you see there several small stars clustered together, in the manner of two clouds a little separated from one another, and somewhat dim.† Now in the middle of them are

★ This clearly indicates Pigafetta's disbelief in a southern continent extending into the tropics.
† The so-called Magellanic clouds.

---

24 January 1521, and so named (Albo); it was perhaps Pukapuka in the northern Tuamotu Archipelago. The second island, sighted eleven days later and named Island of Sharks (*Tiburones*), was one of the Manihiki Archipelago, perhaps Flint Island or Wostock. From 28 November to 16 December 1520 Magellan had coasted northward from Cape Deseado before changing course to northwest.

two stars, not very large nor very bright, and they move slightly.
And these two stars are the Antarctic Pole. Our lodestone always
moved a little toward its Arctic Pole, but it had not so much force as
from its side and its ring. Wherefore, when we were in that gulf, the
captain-general asked all the pilots, always keeping our course, what
sailing track we should prick on the charts. They all replied, By his
course exactly as laid down. And he replied that they pricked it
wrongly (and it was so) and that the needle of navigation should be
adjusted, because it was not receiving so much force as from its side.★
Being in the midst of that gulf, we saw a cross of five very bright
stars right in the west, which were exactly placed one with another.†

CHAPTER XIV

*Navigation of the captain west and northwest, and thence west by south.
Then he comes to an island, whose people robbed him. And he killed many of
them, and burned some of their houses.*

During this time of two months and twelve days, we sailed
between west and northwest, and northwest by west, and
northwest, until we came to the equinoctial line at one hundred and
twenty-two degrees from the line of demarcation. Which line of
demarcation is thirty degrees from the meridian, and the meridian
is three degrees east of Cape Verde. And on this course we passed
near two very rich islands. One is in twenty degrees of latitude
toward the Antarctic Pole, and is called Cipanghu. The other is in
fifteen degrees toward the said pole and is named Sumbdit Pradit.‡
After we had passed the equinoctial line, we sailed between west and

★ This refers to the contemporary practice of correcting the compass for local
magnetic deviation by offsetting the wires from the fleur-de-lis.
† The Southern Cross.
‡ Pigafetta took these two islands from his reading of cosmography or from
hearsay. Cipangu (Japan) was laid down on contemporary world maps,
usually in lat. 15°–35°N. 'Sumbdit Pradit' is supposedly a corruption of
'Septem cidades', the Isle of the Seven Cities.

northwest, and west by north, and then we made two hundred leagues toward the west, and changed course to west by south as far as thirteen degrees toward the Arctic Pole in order to approach the land of Cape Gaticara.* Which cape (under correction of those who have practiced cosmography, for they have not seen it) does not lie where they think, but is to the north in twelve degrees or thereabout.†

After sailing sixty leagues on the aforesaid course, and being in twelve degrees of latitude and one hundred and forty-six of longitude, on Wesnesday the sixth of March we discovered a small island to the northwest, and two others toward the southwest. One of these islands was larger and higher than the other two.‡ And the captain-general wished to approach the largest of these three islands to replenish his provisions. But it was not possible, for the people of those islands entered the ships and robbed us so that we could not protect ourselves from them. And when we wished to strike and take in the sails so as to land, they stole very quickly the small boat called a skiff which was fastened to the poop of the captain's ship. At which he, being very angry, went ashore with forty armed men. And burning some forty or fifty houses with several boats and killing seven men of the said island, they recovered their skiff.

---

* Cape Cattigara, in the Golden Chersonese.
† Magellan's decision to sail so far north, although he knew the Moluccas to lie on the equator, has suggested that he was making for a port of China or for the Ryukyu Islands. His ostensible motive is stated by the Genoese pilot: 'They had information that in the Moluccas there was no food, so he said that he wished to go to the north as much as ten or twelve degrees.'
‡ The high island first sighted was probably Rota, and Guam the large island where landing was made.

CHAPTER XV

The captain's sick men ask for the entrails of the enemy dead. The said enemies follow the captain. Of the men and women, and manners of those people. Of their houses and accoutrements. Of their sports and boats.

S oon after, we left, taking the same course. And before we landed several of our sick men had begged us, if we killed man or woman, to bring them their entrails. For immediately they would be healed. And know that whenever we wounded any of those people with a shaft which entered their body, they looked at it and then marvellously drew it out, and so died forthwith. Soon we left the said island going on our way. And when those people saw that we were departing they followed us for a league in one hundred boats or more and came near our ships, showing us fish and making signs that they wished to give it to us. But they threw stones, then fled away, and in their flight they passed between the boat towed astern and the ship in full sail. But this was done so nimbly and with so much skill that it was a marvel. And we saw some of those women weeping and tearing their hair, and I believe it was for love of those whom we had killed.

Those people live in freedom and as they will, for they have no lord or superior, and they go quite naked and some of them wear a beard. They have long hair down to their waist, and wear small hats after the manner of the Albanians, and these hats are made of palm. Those people are as tall as we, and well built. They worship nothing. And when they are born they are white, then they become tawny, and they have black and red teeth. The women also go naked, but that they cover their nature with a bark as thin and supple as paper, which grows between the wood and the bark of the palm tree. They are handsome and delicate, and whiter than the men, and they have dishevelled hair, very black and hanging down to the ground. They do not go to work in the fields, but do not leave their house, where they make cloth and boxes from palm leaves. Their food is certain fruit called *cochi* [and] *battate*.★ They have birds,

★ Coconuts and sweet potatoes.

figs a palm in length, sugarcanes, and flying fish. Those women anoint their body and their hair with coconut and beneseed oil. And their houses are made of wood covered with planks or boards with fig leaves, which leaves are very large, and the houses are six fathoms wide and have only one story. Their rooms and beds are furnished with mats made of palms and very beautiful, and they lie on palm straw, which is very soft and fine. Those people have no weapons but they use sticks with a fishbone at the tip. They are poor but ingenious, and great thieves. And on this account we called those three islands the Islands of the Thieves.

The pastime of the men and women of that country, and their sport, is to go in their boats to catch those flying fish with hooks made of fishbones. And the form of their boats is painted hereafter, and they are like *fuseleres,*★ but narrower. Some are black and white, and others red. And on the other side of the sail they have a large spar pointed at the top.† Their sails are of palm leaf sewn together like a lateen sail to the right of the tiller. And they have for steering oars certain blades like a shovel. And there is no difference between the stern and the bow in the said boats, which are like dolphins jumping from wave to wave. Those thieves thought (by the signs which they made) that there were no other men in the world but themselves.

CHAPTER XVI

The captain arrives at Zzamal. Nine men come to meet him with gifts. The honour which he paid them. Of the fruit cochi. Palm wine. Ropes for ships. Powder to eat, like bread. Clear and cordial water. Oil, vinegar, and milk made and distilled from the fruit of the palm trees.

On Saturday the sixteenth of March one thousand five hundred and twenty-one we came at daybreak to a high island three hundred leagues from the said Island of Thieves. This island is called Zzamal.‡ And the next day the captain-general decided to anchor

★ *Fisolere,* small oared vessels used on the Venetian lakes for hunting in winter.
† Outrigger.   ‡ Samar, in the Philippines.

at another island,* uninhabited, near the other, to be in greater safety and to take in water there, [and] also to rest for a few days. There he put up two tents on shore for the sick men and had a sow killed for them.

On Monday the eighteenth of March, after dinner, we saw coming toward us a boat with nine men in it. On which the captain-general ordered that no one should move or say anything without his leave. When those people had come to us in that island, forthwith the most ornately dressed of them went toward the captain-general, showing that he was very happy at our coming. And five of the most ornately dressed remained with us, while the others who stayed at the boat went to fetch some who were fishing, and then they all came together. Then the captain, seeing that these people were reasonable, ordered that they be given food and drink, and he presented to them red caps, mirrors, combs, bells, bocasins and other things. And when those people saw the captain's fair dealing, they gave him fish and a jar of palm wine, which they call in their language *vraca*, figs more than a foot long,† and other smaller ones of better flavour, and two coconuts. And then they had nothing more to give him, and they made signs with their hands that in four days they would bring us rice, coconuts and sundry other food.

To declare the kind of fruits named above, know that what they call *cochi* are the fruit borne by the palm trees. And just as we have bread, wine, oil and vinegar in their several kinds, these people have the aforesaid things which come only from the palm trees. And know that wine is obtained from the said palm trees in the following manner. They make an aperture into the heart of the tree at its top which is called *palmito*, from which is distilled along the tree a liquor like white must, which is sweet with a touch of greenness. Then they take canes as thick as a man's leg, by which they draw off this liquor, fastening them to the tree from the evening until next morning, and from the morning to the evening, so that the said liquor comes little by little.

This palm tree bears a fruit, named *cocho* [coconut], which is as

* Suluan, south of Samar.   † Bananas.

large as the head or thereabouts, and its first husk is green and two fingers thick, in which are found certain fibres of which those people make the ropes by which they bind their boats. Under this husk is another, very hard and thicker than that of a nut. This second husk they burn and make of it a powder that is useful to them. And under the said husk there is a white marrow of a finger's thickness. Which they eat fresh with meat and fish, as we do bread, and it has the flavour of an almond, and if it were dried it would make bread. From the centre of this marrow there flows a water which is clear and sweet and very refreshing, and when it stands and settles it congeals and becomes like an apple. And when they wish to make oil they take this fruit called *cocho* and put it in the sun and let the said marrow putrefy and ferment in the water, then they boil it and it becomes oil like butter. When they wish to make vinegar, they let the water of the said *cocho* ferment and put it in the sun, which turns it into vinegar like white wine. From the said fruit milk can also be made, as we proved by experience. For we scraped that marrow, then mixed it with its own water, and being passed through a cloth it became like goat's milk. This kind of palm tree is like the palm that bears dates, but not so knotty. And two of these trees will sustain a family of ten persons. But they do not draw the aforesaid wine always from one tree, but take it for a week from one, and so with the other, for otherwise the trees would dry up. And in this way they last one hundred years.

CHAPTER XVII

Of the island of Zzuluan. The good reception given by the captain to the people of the island. Of the Island of the Water of Good Signs, and other neighbouring islands. Fruits brought to the captain. Of the lord of those people. Of the people named Caphri and of their manners. The author Pigafetta thought to drown. And the captain's further navigation.

These people entered into very great familiarity and friendship with us, and made us understand several things in their language, and the names of some islands which we saw before us. The island in which they lived is called Zzuluan, which is not very large. We took great pleasure with them, because they were merry and conversable. The captain, seeing that they were well disposed, to do them more honour led them to his ship and showed them all his merchandise, namely cloves, cinnamon, pepper, walnut, nutmeg, ginger, mace, gold and all that was in the ship. He also caused his artillery to fire several times, whereat they were much afraid, so that they tried to leap from the ship into the sea. And they made signs that the things which the captain had shown them grew in the places whither we were going. And when they wished to depart, they took leave of the captain and of us with good grace, promising to see us return.

The island where we were is called Humunu.* But because we found there two springs of very clear water, we named it Aquade, that is, the water of good signs. Because in that island we found the first signs of gold. And you find there much white coral, and tall trees which bear fruits smaller than an almond, and they are like pines. There were also many palm trees both good and bad. In that place are several neighbouring islands. Wherefore we called them the Archipelago of St Lazarus. Which region and archipelago are in ten degrees of latitude toward the Arctic Pole, and one hundred and sixty-one degrees of longitude from the line of demarcation.

On Friday the twenty-second of March, the aforesaid people who had promised to return came about noon with two boats loaded with the said cochi, sweet oranges, a jar of palm wine and a cock, to give us to understand that there were fowls in their country, and we purchased all that they brought. The lord of those people was old, and had his face painted, and he wore hanging from his ears golden rings which they call *schione*, and the others wore many gold bracelets and armlets, with a linen kerchief on their head. And we lay eight days in that place, where the captain every day visited the sick men whom he had put ashore on the island to recover. And every day he gave them water from the said cocho fruit, which greatly refreshed them.

* Homonhon, just west of Suluan.

The Island of Thieves, and their boats.

Near the said island, there is another where there are people who have holes in their ears so large that they can pass their arm through. These people, called *Caphri*,* are heathen and go naked, except that round their nature they wear a cloth made of the bark of trees. Howbeit some of the better clad wear cotton cloth, fringed with embroidery of silk done with a needle. Those people are brown, fat and painted, and they anoint themselves with coconut oil and with beneseed oil to protect themselves from the severity of the sun and the wind. They have very black hair hanging to the waist, and they wear small daggers and knives, and lances adorned with gold, and several other things. And their boats are like ours.

On Monday of Holy Week, the twenty-fifth of March and Feast of our Lady, in the afternoon, as we were ready to sail thence, I went on board our ship to fish and, putting my feet on a yard to go down to the store room, my feet slipped from me because it had rained, and I fell into the sea without anyone seeing me. And being about to drown, by chance my left hand caught hold of the foot of the mainsail which was in the sea, and I held on to it and began to call out until someone came to help me and pick me up in the boat. I was succoured, not by my merit, but by the mercy and grace of the fount of pity. This same day we set course between west and southwest, and we passed through the midst of four small islands, namely Cenalo, Hinnangar, Ibusson, and Abarien.†

* These were presumably Negrito aborigines, not Malays.
† Islands lying in Surigao Strait, between Samar and Mindanao: Dinagat (?), Kabugan (?), Hibuson, Cabalian.

CHAPTER XVIII

The captain reaches another island after some of its people had come to him. Their king went there and sent him great gifts which the captain refused. The captain sent a message to the king, who came on board the ship. The honour and the gifts which they exchanged. The friendship of the two. Sport which the captain had made. Pigafetta went ashore with the king. The honour which the king did him. The king's manner of eating and drinking. Their torches. And a king conducted Pigafetta to the ships.

On Thursday the twenty-eighth of March, because during the night we had seen a fire on an island ahead, we came to anchor near the said island,* where we saw a small boat which they call *boloto*, with eight men in it, which came near to the captain-general's ship. Then a slave of his† who was of Zamatra,‡ formerly called Traprobana, spoke to those men at a distance, and they heard him speak and came alongside the ship, but drew off quickly and would not come on board because they mistrusted us. Then the captain, seeing their mistrust, showed them a red cap and other things, which he caused to be tied and fastened on a small plank. Which those of the boat took forthwith and gladly, and then returned to inform their king.

Two hours later, we saw approaching two long boats, which they call *ballanghai*, full of men, and in the larger was their king seated below an awning made of mats. And, when they came near the captain's ship, the said slave spoke to that king, who understood him well. For, in that country, the kings know more languages than the common people do. Then the king ordered some of his men to go to the captain's ship, [telling them] that he would not stir from his boat rather close to us. Which he did, and when his men returned to his boat he immediately departed. The captain made good cheer to those who came to the ship and gave them many things.

* Limasawa, off the south end of Leyte.
† Enrique of Malacca, in the official muster; a slave brought back from the East by Magellan.
‡ Sumatra.

Wherefore the king wished to give the captain a bar of massy gold, of a good size, and a basket full of ginger. But the captain, thanking him greatly, refused to accept the present. Then in the evening we came with the ships near to the captain's house.

On Good Friday, the captain sent ashore the said slave, our interpreter, to the king, requesting him to cause, in return for his money, some provisions to be given for his ships, telling him that he had come into his country, not as an enemy, but as a friend. The king, hearing that, came with seven or eight men in a boat, and boarded the ship, and embraced the captain, and gave him three porcelain jars covered with leaves and full of raw rice, and two *orades*,* which are fairly large fish of the kind described above, and he gave him also some other things. The captain gave this king a robe of red and yellow cloth, made in the Turkish fashion, and a very fine red cap, and to some of the people he gave knives, and to others mirrors. Then he had a collation served for them. And by the said interpreter he caused the king to be told that he wished to be with him *cassi cassi*,† that is, brothers. To which the king replied that he too wished to be the same with him.

After that the captain showed him cloths of divers colours, and linen, coral and many other goods, and all the artillery, several pieces of which he caused to be fired before his eyes, whereby the king was greatly astonished. This done, the said captain had one of his soldiers armed in plate armour and put him in the middle of three companions who struck him with swords and daggers. Which thing the king thought very strange. And the captain caused him to be told by the slave interpreter that one man clad in plate armour was worth one hundred of his men, and the king replied that it was true. And the captain gave him to understand that in each ship were two hundred such as that man. He showed him also a great number of swords, of cuirasses and bucklers, and then he made two of his men exercise at swordplay before the king. And he showed him the marine chart and the compass of his ship, telling him how

---

* Dorado.

‡ *Casicasi*, the ceremony of blood brotherhood among Malays.

he had found the strait [by which] to come hither, and of the time which he had spent in coming, also how he had not seen any land. At which the king marvelled. Lastly, the captain asked whether it would please the king that two of the captain's men should go with him to the country where he lived, that the king might show them other things of his country. To which the king agreed, and I went with one other.

When I had set foot on shore, this king raised his hands to heaven, then he turned toward us, and we did likewise. After this he took me by the hand, and one of his more notable men took my companion, and he led us under a place covered with reeds, where there was a *ballanghai*, that is to say, a boat eighty feet or thereabouts in length, like a foist.* And there we seated ourselves with the said king on the poop of that boat, always speaking with him by signs. And his men stood round us with their swords, spears, and bucklers. The king then sent for a dish of pork's flesh, and wine. And the manner of their drinking is this. They raise their hands to heaven first, then take the drinking vessel in their right hand and extend the fist of their left hand toward the company. Which the king did, offering me his fist, with which I thought he would strike me. But I did likewise toward him. Thus with this ceremony and other signs of friendship we banqueted, [and] then supped with him. I ate flesh on Good Friday, being unable to do otherwise. And before the hour of supper I gave the king some things which I had brought. There I wrote down several things as they call them in their language. And when the king and the others saw me writing, and I told them their way of speaking, all were astonished.

Meanwhile, the hour of supper being come, two large porcelain dishes were brought, one full of rice, and the other of pork's flesh with its broth and gravy. We supped with the same signs and ceremonies. Then we went to the king's palace, constructed and built as it were of thatch, and it was covered with leaves of fig and of palm. It was built up from the ground on thick high posts, and we had to climb up to it by steps and ladders. The king made us sit on a reed

* A light oared galley or barge.

mat, with our legs folded like tailors. And after half an hour a dish of fish, roasted in pieces, was brought, and ginger freshly gathered, and wine. The eldest son of the king (who was the prince) came where we were. And the king told him to seat himself beside us, which he did. Then two dishes were brought, one of fish in its sauce and the other of rice. And this was in order that we might eat with the said prince. And my companion made so good cheer in drinking and eating that he became intoxicated. For candles or torches they use gum of a tree called *anime*, wrapped in leaves of palm or of fig.* The king signed to us that he wished to go to bed, and he left the prince with us, with whom we lay down on a mat of reeds, and cushions and pillows of leaves.

Next morning the king came and took me by the hand, and we went thus to the place where we had supped in order to breakfast, but the boat came to fetch us. And before parting the king very happily kissed our hands, and we kissed his. And a brother of his, king of another island, came with us, accompanied by three men. And the captain-general kept him to dine with him, and we gave him several things.

CHAPTER XIX

Of the king Raia Calambu, brother of the first king called Raia Siaiu. Of his accoutrements, and of his country. The mass of Easter Day and other ceremonies. Of the two aforesaid kings. Of a cross set up by their consent. Interrogation between one of the kings and the captain. The said king's offer to the captain. That king wished to guide the captain. What he did.

In the island of that king who came to the ship are mines of gold, which is found by digging from the earth large pieces as large as walnuts and eggs. And all the vessels he uses are likewise [of gold], as are also some parts of his house, which was well fitted in the fashion of the country. And he was the most handsome person whom we saw among those peoples. He had very black hair to his shoulders, with a silk cloth on his head, and two large gold rings hanging from

* Banana.

his ears. He wore a cotton cloth, embroidered with silk, which covered him from his waist to his knees. At his side he had a dagger with a long handle, and all of gold, the sheath of which was of carved wood. Withal he wore on his person perfumes of storax and benzoin. He was tawny and painted all over. His island is called Butuan and Calaghan.* And when the two kings wish to visit each other, they go hunting on the island where we were. Of these kings, the aforesaid painted one is named Raia Calambu, and the other Raia Siaiu.

On Sunday the last day of March, and Easter Day, the captain early in the morning sent the chaplain ashore to celebrate mass. And the interpreter went with him to tell the king that we were not landing to dine with him, but only to hear mass. Hearing this the king sent two dead pigs. And when the hour for saying mass came, the captain with fifty men went ashore, not in armour, but only with swords, and dressed as honourably as it was possible for each man to do. And, before we reached shore with the boats, our ships fired six shots as a sign of peace. When we landed, the two kings were there, and they received our captain kindly, and put him in the centre between the two of them. Then we went to the place prepared for saying mass, which was not far from the shore. And before mass began the captain threw much rose muscat water over those two kings. Then when it came to the offering of the mass, those two kings went to kiss the cross as we did, but they did not offer anything. And at the elevation of the body of our Lord they knelt as we did and worshipped our Lord with clasped hands. And the ships fired all their artillery at the elevation of our Lord's body. After mass was said, each did the work of a good Christian, receiving our Lord.

Then the captain ordered swordplay by his men, in which the kings took great pleasure. This done, he had a cross brought, with the nails and the crown, to which those kings did reverence. And the captain caused them to be told that these things which he showed them were the insignia of the Emperor his lord and master, by whom he was charged and commanded to set them up in all the

* Butuan and Caraga, districts in the eastern part of the island of Mindanao.

places where he should go and travel. And he told them that he wished to set them up in their country for their benefit, so that if any ships of Spain came afterward to those islands, they seeing the said cross would know that we had been there. And by this token they would do them no harm, and if they took any of their men, being immediately shown this sign, they would let them go. Moreover, the captain told them that it was necessary that the cross be set up at the top of the highest mountain in their country, so that every day, seeing the said cross, they might worship it, and that, if they did this, not thunder, lightning, nor tempest could harm them.

Those kings thanked the captain and said that they would be willing to do this. Then he caused them to be asked whether they were Moors or heathen, and in what they believed. And they replied that they worshipped no other thing but they clasped their hands, looking up to heaven, and called upon their god *Aba*. Hearing this, the captain was very glad, and seeing this, the first king raised his hands to heaven, and said that he desired if it were possible to manifest to the captain the love which he bore him. And the interpreter asked him why there was in that place so little to eat. The king replied that he did not sojourn in that place except when he went hunting, or to see his brother, but that he lived in another island, where he had all his family. Then the captain caused him to be asked whether he had any enemies who made war on him, for, if he had any, he would go with his men and ships to destroy them in order to bring them into submission to him. The king in reply said that there were two islands whose people were his enemies, but that this was not the season at which to go and attack them. And the captain said that, if God granted him to return again into that country, he would bring so many men that he would bring them by force into submission to the king. This done, he caused the interpreter to tell them that he was going to dinner, and that afterward he would return to have the cross set up at the top of the mountain. And the two kings said that they were content, and at this, embracing the captain, they departed together.

After dinner we returned all in our doublets, and we went together with the two kings to the centre of the highest mountain which we could find, and there the cross was set up. Then those two kings and the captain rested, and while discoursing he had them asked where was the best port to find provisions. And they replied that there were three: namely, Ceylon, Zzubu, and Calaghan.* But that Zzubu was the largest, and of the best trade. Then those kings offered to give him pilots to sail to those ports, wherefor he thanked them and decided to go thither. For his evil destiny willed it thus.†
And after the cross was erected on that mountain, every man said a Pater Noster and Ave Maria, worshipping it. And those kings did likewise. Then we descended and went to the place where their boats were. And those kings sent for the fruit named *cochi* and other things to make a collation and refresh ourselves.

The captain, desiring to leave on the morrow, asked the king for the pilots to guide him to the aforesaid ports. For he had promised and given assurance that he would treat them like himself, and that he would leave one of his men as a hostage. And they replied that whenever he would they were at his command. But in the night the first king changed his mind, for on the morning of the next day, when we were ready to depart, the said king sent to tell the captain that for love of him he wished to go himself to guide him to those ports and be his pilot, and that he would wait for two days until he had had his rice gathered, and other things which he had to do, and praying him that to be done sooner the captain should lend him some of his men. And the captain agreed to this, and sent him some men. But the kings ate and drank so much that they slept all day. And some, to excuse them, said that they were sick. Wherefore we did nothing that day. But the two days following we laboured. One of those men brought us a plate of rice with eight or ten figs tied together to exchange them for a knife, which was worth at the

* The islands of Panaon, to the east, and Cebu, to the west of Limasawa, and the Caraga district of Mindanao, to the southeast.
† Pigafetta, writing his narrative after his return to Europe, anticipates Magellan's death.

most four *quattrini*.★ And the captain, seeing that that man wanted nothing but a knife, called him and put his hand in his purse, and offered him a *real* for that thing. But he refused. Then he was shown a ducat, and would accept that even less. At length he was offered a double ducat, but he wanted nothing but a knife, which the captain caused to be given to him. Not long after, one of our men went ashore to fetch water, and one of the people aforesaid wished to give him a pointed crown of massy gold for six large pieces of glass. But the captain would not allow such an exchange to be made, in order that those people should know that we prized and held in more regard our merchandise than their gold.

CHAPTER XX

Manner of living and accoutrements of the aforesaid men and women. Of the food by which they refresh themselves. Of the produce of that island. In what position it is from the Arctic Pole. Other islands by which the captain passed. Of an island to which he came. Of several birds and animals in that island. Of a bird and of the hatching of its eggs. The king of Mazzaua went with the captain, and at length came on board the captain's ship.

Those people are heathens, and go naked, and are painted, and wear a piece of cloth made from a tree like a linen round their private parts, and they are great drinkers. The women are clad in tree cloth from the waist down. And they have black hair hanging down to the ground, and they wear certain gold rings in their ears. Those people chew most of the time a fruit which they call *areca*,† which is something like a pear, and they cut it into four quarters, then wrap it in leaves of its tree, called *betre*,‡ and they are like mulberry leaves. And mixing it with a little lime, after they have chewed it for a long time, they spit and throw it out. And from this they afterward have a very red mouth. And many people use the said fruit because it greatly refreshes them, for the country is so hot

★ *Quattrino*, an Italian copper coin struck in the fifteenth century.
† Betel. ‡ Betel pepper.

that they could not live without it. In that island there is great quantity of dogs, cats, pigs, poultry and goats, of rice, ginger, coconuts, figs,* oranges, lemons, millet, wax and gold mines. That island is in the latitude of nine and two thirds degrees toward the Arctic Pole, and in the longitude of one hundred and sixty-two from the line of demarcation. And from the other island, where we found the springs of fresh water, it is twenty-five leagues distant. And that island is called Mazzaua.†

We remained seven days in this place, then we laid course to the south-west, passing through five islands, namely, Ceylon, Bohol, Canighan, Baibai, and Gatighan.‡ In this island of Gatighan are a kind of birds called *barbastigly*, who are as large as eagles.§ Of which we killed a single one, because it was late, which we ate, and it had the taste of a fowl. There are also in that island pigeons, doves, turtledoves, parrots and certain black birds as large as a fowl, with a long tail.|| They lay eggs as large as those of a goose, which they bury a good cubit deep under the sand in the sun, and so they are hatched by the great heat made by the warm sand. And when those birds are hatched they emerge. And those eggs are good to eat.

From the said island of Mazzaua to that of Gatighan it is twenty leagues. And leaving Gatighan we went westward. But the king of Mazzaua could not follow us, wherefore we awaited him near three islands, namely Polo, Ticobon, and Pozzon.¶ When the king arrived, he was astonished at our sailing, and the captain-general made him come on board his ship with some of his principal men, at which they were very pleased. And so we went to Zzubu, which is fifteen leagues distant from Gatighan.

---

* Bananas.   † Limasawa.

‡ The islands of Panaon (south of Leyte), Bohol (southwest of Leyte) and Canigao; the district of Baybay (in central Leyte); and the island of Apit or Himuquetan (?). The ships were sailing north through the Canigao Channel, along the west coast of Leyte.

§ These were 'flying foxes' or large fruit-eating bats. || Megapodes.

¶ The Camote Islands, west of Leyte: Poro, Pasijan, and Poson.

CHAPTER XXI

The captain comes to the port of Zzubu, and sends some of his men to the king, who inquired after the captain's coming. The king demands tribute. A Moorish merchant takes it. Behaviour of the king to the captain's men, and the honour which he did them. And confederacy and peace between the said king and the captain.

On Sunday the seventh of April, about noon, we entered the port of Zzubu, having passed by many villages where we saw some houses which were built on trees. And nearing the principal town the captain-general ordered all the ships to put out their flags. Then we lowered the sails as is done when one is about to fight, and fired all the artillery, at which the people of those places were in great fear. The captain sent a young man, his foster son, with the interpreter to the king of that island of Zzubu. And when they came to the town they found a great number of men and their king with them, all frightened by the artillery which had been fired. But the interpreter reassured them, saying that it was the habit and custom to fire the artillery on arrival in ports, as a token of peace and friendship. And also it was to do more honour to the king of the country that all the artillery had been fired. The king and all his people were reassured, and then he caused one of his principal men to speak and to ask what we were in search of. And the interpreter told him that his master was a captain of the greatest king in the world, and that by his command he was going to discover the islands of Molucca. Yet, for that he had heard, in the way by which he came, and especially from the King of Mazzaua, report of his honourable and good fame, he had wished to pass by his country in order to visit him, and to have also some replenishment of provisions for his merchandise. The king replied that he was welcome, but that it was the custom that all ships arriving in his port or country should pay tribute. And but four days before a ship called *iunco*,* from Ciama,† loaded with gold and slaves, had paid him her tribute. And to prove

* A junk.   † Siam, or 'Champa' (Cambodia).

the truth of what he said, he showed them a merchant of the said Ciama, who had remained there to do trade in gold and slaves.

The interpreter told him that the captain, as captain of so great a king as his, would not pay tribute to any lord in the world, and that if he desired peace he should have peace, and if he desired war, war he should have. Then the aforesaid merchant replied to the king in his own language, *Cata raia chita*, which is to say, Have good care, O king, what you do, for these men are of those who have conquered Calicut, Malacca, and all India the Greater. If you give them good reception and treat them well, it will be well for you, but if you treat them ill, so much the worse it will be for you, as they have done at Calicut and at Malacca.

The interpreter, who understood all this discourse, told them that his master's king was even more powerful in ships and by land than the King of Portugal, and he declared that he was the King of Spain and Emperor of all Christendom. Wherefore, if he did not wish to be his friend and treat his subjects well, he would send to him again so many men against him that he would destroy him. Then the king answered that he would speak with his council, and would give his reply on the following day. This done, the king caused to be served a meal of several dishes, all of meat, in porcelain dishes, with many jars of wine. And when the meal was over, our men returned and told all to the captain. And the King of Mazzaua (being in the captain's ship), who was considered as the first king after the King of Zzubu, and lord of many islands, went ashore to relate to the said king the honourable character and courtesy of our captain.

On Monday morning, our notary went with the interpreter into the said town of Zzubu, and the king, accompanied by the leading men of his kingdom, came to the square, where he made our men sit down near him, and asked them whether there was more than one captain in all the ships, and whether he desired that the king pay tribute to the Emperor his master. To which our men replied, no, but that the captain wished only to trade in the things which he carried with the people of his country, and not with others. Thereupon the king said that he was content, and that if the captain wished to be his friend, as a greater token of love he would send him a little of his blood, from the right arm, and that the captain should do likewise. And our men answered that they would do it. Moreover he told them that all the captains who came into his country had been accustomed to make him a present, and he to them, and that they should therefore ask their captain if he would observe the custom. And our men said, yes, but that, since he wished to maintain the custom, he should begin by making a present, and afterward the captain would do what was due.

CHAPTER XXII

The King of Mazzaua came with a Moorish merchant to the ships, and afterward the prince, nephew of the king. The reception which the captain gave them, and some inquiries. The pleasure which they took in the captain's words, and on the faith of Jesus Christ. The prince and those with him promised to be Christians. Remonstrances which the captain made to them thereon. Peace made between the king and the captain. And the presents which the king gave to the captain, and the captain to the prince and to his men.

On the Tuesday morning following, the King of Mazzaua with the Moor came to the ship, and greeted the captain on behalf of the King of Zzubu, and told him that that king was preparing as many provisions as he could to make him a present of them, and that after dinner he would send two of his nephews with other notable men to make peace with him. Then the captain had one of his men armed with his own harness, and made it known that we should all fight armed in this way. At this the Moorish merchant was much astonished. But the captain told him that he was not to be afraid, and that our weapons were mild to our friends, and sharp to our enemies, and that, just as linen absorbs a man's sweat, so our weapons destroy the enemies of our faith. And the captain said this to the Moor, because he was more intelligent than the others, that he might tell all to the King of Zzubu.

After dinner the king's nephew (who was a prince) with the King of Mazzaua, the Moor, the governor and the chief constable and eight of the chief men came to the ship, to make peace with us. The captain-general was seated on a red velvet chair, and near him were the leading men of the ships seated on chairs covered in leather. Then the captain had those men asked by the interpreter whether their custom was to speak in secret or in public, and whether the prince who had come with them had authority to make peace. And they replied, yes, and that they would speak in public, and that they had authority to make peace. The captain spoke long on the matter of peace, and prayed God that He would confirm it in heaven. Those people replied that they had never heard such words as the captain had spoken to them, and took great pleasure in hearing them. Then the captain, seeing that those people listened gladly to what was said to them, and that they gave good answers, began further to tell them many good things to induce them to become Christians.

After several remarks the captain asked them who succeeded to the king when he died. And they replied that the king had no son, but many daughters, and that this prince who was his nephew had as wife the king's eldest daughter, and for love of her he was called prince. And they said moreover that, when the father and the mother were old, no more account was taken of them, but the children commanded them. Then the captain told them how God had made the heaven, the earth, and the sea, and all other things in the world, and that he had commanded every man to do honour and obedience to his father and mother, and that any man who did otherwise was condemned to eternal fire. And he told how we were descended from Adam and Eve, our first parents, and how we had immortal souls. Then he showed them several other things touching our faith, which those people heard gladly, and begged the captain to leave them two men, or at least one, to teach them and unfold the Christian faith, and that they would give them good company and great honour. To which the captain replied that at this time he could not leave any of his men, but that, if they wished to be Christians, his priest would baptize them, and that another time he would bring priests and preachers to teach them his faith. Then they replied that they wished first to speak to their king, and then would become Christians.

Each of us wept for the joy that we had at the goodwill of those people. And the captain told them that they should not become Christians for fear of us, or in order to please us, but that if they wished to become Christians, it should be with a good heart and for the love of God. For that, if they did not become Christians, we should show them no displeasure. But that those who became Christians would be more regarded and better treated than the others. Then all cried out together with one voice that they wished to become Christians not for fear, nor to pleaseus, but of their own free will. Then the captain said that if they became Christians he would leave them weapons which Christians use, and that his king had ordered him to do this. And he showed them that they could not have intercourse with their women without great sin, because they were heathen. And he assured them that since they were Christians, the devil would no longer appear to them except at the point and extremity of death. Lastly they said that they could not reply to so many fair words which he spoke to them, but they put themselves in his hands, and that he should treat them as his own servants. Then the captain with tears in his eyes embraced them, and taking the prince's hand and that of the king, he told and promised them by the faith which he bore to God, and to his master the Emperor, and by the habit of St James which he wore, that he would cause perpetual peace to be between them and the King of Spain. Then the prince and the others promised likewise.

After peace was concluded, the captain had a collation prepared for them. And that prince and the King of Mazzaua who was with him presented to the captain on behalf of his king large boxes full of rice, swine, goats and poultry. And they asked the said captain to forgive them in that their present was not so fair as was proper for him. The captain gave to the said prince very fine cloth, a red cap and a quantity of glass, and a gilt glass cup. For glass is much prized in that country. To the King of Mazzaua he gave no present, for that he had before given him a robe and several other things. To the people of the said prince he gave divers things. Then the captain sent by me and another to the King of Zzubu a robe of yellow and violet silk after the fashion of a Turkish jubbah, a very fine red cap and certain pieces of glass, and he had it all put in a silver dish, and two gilt cups.

CHAPTER XXIII

Of the King of Zzubu and his accoutrements. Of the presents which the king sent him. Of the prince, the king's nephew. Of his four daughters. Of their accoutrements and instruments. Two of the captain's men, who had died, buried in the town of Zzubu. The captain's merchandise carried into the town, on which the king placed a guard. Manner of living of the people of Zzubu. Of the Cornioles which kill the whale. Exchange of merchandise between one and another. And the platform set up to baptize the king and his people.

When we had come to the town, we found the King of Zzubu at his palace, seated on the ground on a mat of palms, with many people. He was quite naked, except for a linen cloth covering his private parts, and round his head a very loose cloth, embroidered with silk. Round his neck he had a very heavy and rich chain, and in his ears two gold rings hung with precious stones. He was a short man, and fat, and had his face painted with fire in divers patterns. He ate on the ground from another palm mat, and then he was eating turtle eggs on two porcelain dishes, and he had four jars full of palm wine, which he drank with reed pipes. We made reverence to him as we presented what the captain had sent him, and we told him, by the mouth of the interpreter, that it was not in return for the present which he had given to the captain, but for the love which he bore him. Then we clothed him in the robe, put the cap on his head, and kissed the glasses that I presented to him and that he accepted. Then the king made us eat those eggs and drink from the said reeds. And meanwhile his people told him all the good words and assurances of peace and faith that had been given to them.

Then the king wished to retain us for supper, but we made our excuses, and on this we took leave of him.

The prince, nephew of this king, led us to his house, and showed us four girls who were playing on four very strange and very sweet instruments, and their manner of playing was rather musical. One played on a taborin after our fashion, but it stood on the ground. Another was striking, with a thick stick wrapped at the head with palm leaf, the bottom of two instruments shaped like a long taborin. Another was striking another larger instrument in the same manner. And the last, with two other similar instruments, one in one hand and the other in the other. And they struck in harmony, making a very sweet sound. These girls were very beautiful, and almost white and as tall as ours. They were naked, except that from the waist to the knees they wore a garment made from the said palm cloth, covering their nature. And some were quite naked, having long black hair and a small veil round their head, and they go always unshod. The prince made us dance with three of them who were quite naked. And we had refreshment there, and then we returned to the ship. Those taborins are of metal, and they are made in the country of the Sinus Magnus, which is China. There they use them as we do bells, and they are called *aghon*.

On Wednesday morning (since the night before one of our men had died) the interpreter and I (by the captain's command) went to ask the said king for a place where we could bury the dead man. We found the king in a large company, and after paying him the honour due to him, we told him of the death of our man, and that the captain requested that he be interred. And he replied, that if he and his people were ready to obey our master, all the more ought his land and country to be subject to him. And then we said that we wished to consecrate and bless the grave in our manner, and set up a cross above it. That lord said that he was content, and that he himself would worship that cross as we did. The dead man was buried in the middle of the square as honourably as possible, performing the aforesaid ceremonies, to give them a good example, and in the evening we buried another. That done, we carried a quantity of merchandise into the said king's town, and put it in a house. And he took it in his charge, promising that no ill or wrong should be done to the king. Four of our men were chosen to sell and despatch the said merchandise.

Those people live in justice, having weights and measures, and loving peace, and they are men of goodwill. They have wooden scales in the fashion of Pardeça,* for weighing merchandise. Their houses are built of wood, and of planks and bamboo, raised on piers, and are high so that you must climb up to them by ladders. Their rooms are like ours, and below them they keep their cattle, such as pigs, goats, and fowls. In the said island of that king there are animals with a shell, named *cornioles*, beautiful in appearance, which cause whales to die. For the whale swallows them alive. Then when they are in its body they come out of their shell and eat the whale's heart. And these animals called cornioles have teeth, and a black skin, and their shell is white, and their flesh is good to eat, and they are called *laghan*.

The Friday following we showed those people a shop full of our merchandise, which was of divers strange sorts, at which they marvelled. For metal, iron, and other large wares, they gave us gold, and for the other smaller and meaner goods rice, pigs, goods and other provision. And they gave us ten weights of gold for fourteen pounds of iron. Each weight is a ducat and a half. The captain did not wish us to take a great quantity of gold, lest the sailors should sell what they had too cheaply for greed of gold, and he should therefore be constrained to do likewise with his merchandise. For he wished to sell it at a better rate.

On Saturday following, he caused a platform to be built on the square, decked with tapestry and palm branches, because the king had promised our captain to become a Christian on Sunday. And he told him that he should have no fear when our artillery fired on that day. For it was the custom to discharge it on festivals without firing stones or other shot.

* *par de ça*, i.e. the Languedoïl, or that part of France north of the Loire (as distinct from *par de là*, or Languedoc).

CHAPTER XXIV

The captain's order of march to the town of Zzubu. The king embraced him.
Instruction of the king in our faith. The captain's promises to the king. The
king, the prince, the King of Mazzaua, the Moor, and several others were
baptized. Of their names. Mass said. Of the baptism of the queen and other
ladies. A great number of people baptized. Of the queen. All those of the
island baptized. A village burned. Mass said every day. The queen at the
mass. And an image which the captain gave them.

On Sunday morning the fourteenth day of April we went ashore,
being forty men, of whom two armed men marched in front,
with the banner of our Emperor. And as we landed the ships discharged all their artillery. Then for the fear that the people of the
country had they fled hither and thither. The captain and the king
embraced each other. And the captain said to that king that it was
not the custom to carry the royal banner ashore unless with fifty
men, as they were, and with the aforesaid two men armed, and fifty
hackbuts. But that for the great love he bore him he had caused it to
be brought. Then very joyfully we went up to the platform, where
the king and the captain were seated on two chairs, one covered
with red velvet, and the other with violet. The leading men were
on cushions, and the others on mats after the fashion of the country.

Then the captain began to speak to the king through the interpreter, to initiate him into the faith of Jesus Christ, [saying] that he
thanked God for having inspired him to become a Christian, and
that he would vanquish his enemies more than before. And the king
replied that he wished to be a Christian, but that some of his chief
men would not obey him, saying that they were men as he was.
Then our captain summoned all the chief men of the king, and told
them that if they did not obey the king (as he himself did) he would
have them all killed, and would give all their goods to the king. And
they all replied that they would obey him.

Then the captain told the king that if he went to Spain he would
return another time with so great a power that he would make him

the greatest king in all those parts, because he was the first who had agreed to become a Christian. And the king, raising his hands to heaven, thanked him, and begged him to leave some of his men, that he and his people might be better instructed in the faith. To which the captain answered that to content him he would leave behind two men, but that he wished to take away with him two children of the chief men, to have them taught our language, that after their return they might be able to say and relate to others the matters of Spain.

This said, the captain set up a great cross in the centre of the square, exhorting the king that, if he wished to be a good Christian (as he had said the day before), he must burn all the idols of his country, and set up a cross in their place, and that everyone should worship it daily on his knees, and with clasped hands held up to heaven. And he showed him how every day the sign of the cross must be made. And he told him that every hour (at least in the morning) they must come to worship this cross on their knees, and that they should confirm with good works what they had said and promised. To which the king and all his people answered that they wished to obey the captain's commands, and do all that he should tell them. Then the captain told him that he was clad all in white to show them the pure love that he bore them. And they all replied that they knew not how to answer him for his fair words. And so with these good words the captain took the king by the hand, and they went up on the platform. And when he came to baptize him, he told him that he would name him Dam Charles, as was the name of the Emperor his lord. The prince he named Dam Ferrand, after the brother of the said Emperor. To another chief he gave the name Fernand, like himself. And the King of Mazzaua, John. To the Moor he gave the name Christopher. And to each of the others a name of his choice. So were baptized, before the mass, fifty men. Mass having been heard, the captain invited to dinner with him the king and the other chief men, but the king excusing himself refused. But he accompanied the captain to the shore. And at their arrival the ships discharged all the artillery. Then, embracing one another, they took their leave.

After dinner, our chaplain and some others of us went on shore to baptize the queen. And she came with forty ladies, and we led them on to the platform, then we caused her to sit on a cushion, and her women about her, until the priest was ready. Meanwhile we showed her a lady carved in wood, holding her child (which was very well made), and a cross. The sight of this gave her a greater wish to be a Christian and asking for baptism she was baptized, and named Joanna, like the Emperor's mother. The prince's wife, the daughter of that queen, had the name Katherine, the Queen of Mazzaua Ysabeau, and all the others had each her name.

That day we baptized eight hundred persons, men, women, and children. The queen was young and beautiful, covered with a white and black cloth. She had very red mouth and nails, and wore on her head a large hat made of palm leaves, with a crown above made of the same leaves, after the fashion of the Pope's. And she never goes into any place without one of these crowns. Then she begged us to give her that wooden image, to put in place of the idols. Which we did.* And then she went away. In the evening, the king and the queen with several of their people came to the seashore, and the captain caused the large pieces of artillery to be fired, in which they took great pleasure. The captain and the king called one another brother. And this king was formerly named Raia Humabon. And from that time, before a week had passed, all those of this island, and of some others, were baptized. And we burned a village which refused to obey the king or us. This was in an island near to that one. There we set up the cross, because those people were heathen. And if they had been Moors we should have put up a column, as a sign of greater achievement, for these Moors are more difficult to convert than the heathen.

During those days, the captain-general went daily ashore to hear mass, and he told the king many things the better to instruct him and confirm him in the faith. And the queen came one day in great

* This Flemish statuette, with the crosses set up by Magellan, was recovered on 28 April 1565 by the Spanish conquistador Miguel López de Legazpi. It is still preserved in the Augustinian church on Cebu.

state to hear mass, and three maidens went before her, each carrying a hat in her hand. And the queen was clad in black and white, wearing on her head a very loose linen cloth embroidered with gold thread. This cloth covered her to her shoulders, and over this cloth she had her hat. She was followed by several women, all naked and unshod, except that their shameful parts were covered by a cloth made from the palm tree, and round their head they wore another small linen cloth, with their hair hanging down. The queen, having made reverence to the altar, sat down on a cushion embroidered with silk. And before mass began, the captain threw rose muscat water over her, and also over her maidens, at which they were very joyful. The captain, knowing that the wooden image greatly pleased the queen, gave it to her, saying that she should have it instead of her idols, for that it was the memorial and representation of the Son of God. And hearing this, the queen accepted it, and warmly thanked the captain for it.

CHAPTER XXV

The king and his brother swore fealty to the King of Spain. Miracle of a sick man healed. Idols burned by him. And of the towns and the names of their lords in that island.

One day, before mass, the captain-general caused the king to come clad in his silk robe, with the chief men of his city, the brother of the king (who was the prince's father) named Bendara,* another brother of the king, called Cadaio, and several others, and he made them all swear to obey the king, and the king to be faithful to the King of Spain. And they all swore. Then the captain drew his sword before the image of Our Lady, telling the king that, when one swore in this manner, one must sooner die than break such an oath. And so much did the captain that the king swore by that image, by the life of the Emperor, and by his habit, to be always faithful and subject

* Bendara is not a personal name but the title of one of the principal officers of the king's government.

to the Emperor. All this being done, the captain gave the king a red velvet chair, saying that when he wished to go anywhere, he was to have it borne before him by some of those most nearly related to him, showing him the manner of carrying it. To which the king replied that he would do this with a good heart for love of him. Then he told the captain that he was having a jewel made to give him. This was two very large gold rings to be fastened and hung in the ears; two to wear on the arms above the elbows; and two others to wear on the feet above the heels; and the other precious stones to adorn and deck the ears. These are the most beautiful ornaments which the kings of that country can wear. And those people always go unshod, with a cloth hanging down to the knees.

One day the captain-general asked the king and the others why it was that they did not burn their idols, as they had promised him when they became Christians, and why they sacrificed so much flesh to them. And they answered that they did this not for themselves, but for a sick man, that the idols might give him health. And he had not spoken for four days, and he was the prince's brother, and the most valiant and wise man in the whole island. Then the captain said that they should burn the idols and believe in Jesus Christ, and that if the sick man had himself baptized, he would immediately be cured. And that if this was not true they could cut off his head. The king replied that he would do so, for he believed truly in Jesus Christ. Whereon we made a procession from the square to the sick man's house, as well as we could, and there we found him unable to speak or to move. Then we baptized him, and two wives whom he had, and ten maidens. Then the captain had him asked how he was, and he at once spoke, and said that by the grace of our God he was very well. And this was a very manifest miracle in our time.

When the captain heard him speak, he greatly thanked God, and immediately caused him to drink some almond milk which he had had prepared for him. Then he sent him a mattress, a pair of sheets, a blanket of yellow cloth and a pillow. And every day, until he was well, he sent him almond milk, rosewater, oil of roses, and some sweet preserves, so that before five days had passed he had begun to walk. That sick man, seeing his recovery, caused an idol to be burned, which some old women had hidden in his house, in the presence of the king and of all the people. And he caused several tabernacles on the seashore to be dismantled and demolished, where they ate the consecrated flesh. And the people themselves cried out, Castille Castille, as they destroyed and pulled down the said tabernacles. And he said that if God granted him life, he would burn as many idols as he could find, were it in the chamber of the king himself. These idols are of hollow wood without any back parts. They have the arms open, the feet turned up, with legs open, and a large face with four very large teeth like those of wild boars, and they are painted all over.

In that island are several towns. Their names, and those of the principal lords, are these: Cinghapola, Cilaton, Ciguibucan, Cimaningha, Cimaticat, Cicambul. Another Mandaui, and its lord Lambuzzan. Another Cotcot, and its lord Acibagalen. Another Puzzo, and its lord Apanoan. Another Lalen, and its lord Theteu. Another Lulutan, and its lord Tapan. Another Cilumay, and again Lubucun. All these towns and their lords are subject to the king, and each gives him provisions and pays tribute. And after that island of Zzubu is another named Mattan★ which formed the port where we were. And the name of its town was Mattan, and its lords Zzula and Cilapulapu. And the village which we burned was in that island, and its name was Bullaia.

★ Mactan, a small island lying in the Bohol Strait off the port of Sebu and forming a sheltered anchorage.

CHAPTER XXVI

Ceremonies which they use in killing pigs. Of the shameful member of the men. Ceremonies for a dead man. And of a bird which comes there by night.

hat your very illustrious lordship★ may know the ceremonies which those people use in the consecration of pigs, know that first they sound large *borchies*, instruments so named, which are taborins or disks of brass. Then three large dishes are brought, two with roses and rice and boiled millet, wrapped in leaves with roast fish, the other with cloth of Cambaia and two palm flags. Then a Cambaia cloth is spread on the ground. Then two very old women come, each having a bamboo trumpet in her hand. And when they are on that cloth, they make reverence to the Sun, then wrap themselves in those cloths. And one of them puts on her forehead a kerchief with two horns which she makes of it, and takes another in her hand, with which, dancing and sounding the said instrument, she calls on the Sun. The other takes one of those flags and dances, blowing on her trumpet, and the other dances with her, both saying many things to the Sun. Then she with the kerchief takes the other flag and lets go the kerchief. And the two, blowing their trumpets, dance for some time round the bound pig. She of the horns continues to speak secretly to the Sun, and the other answers her.

Then she of the horns is given a glass of wine, and dancing and saying certain words the other answers her. And making as if to drink the wine four or five times, she sprinkles it round the pig's heart, then turns round immediately to dance. Then she is given a very sharp lance which she waves and shakes. And both continuing to say some words, she who holds the lance, dancing and singing, four or five times makes as if to thrust it into the pig's heart, and then with a sudden abrupt motion pierces his heart from side to side, and forthwith she crouches and stops the wound with grass. She who killed the pig places a burning torch in her mouth, biting on it

★ Villiers de l'Isle-Adam, Grand Master of Rhodes, to whom Pigafetta's narrative was addressed.

and holding it between her teeth, still flaming, during this ceremony. The other who carries the trumpet dips it in the pig's blood
and then goes to touch and smear with it the foreheads first of their
husbands, and then of others; but she never came to us. This done,
they undress, and go to eat the food which is on the dishes, to which
they invite only women. Then the pig is skinned in the fire. And no
one but the old women consecrates the pig's flesh. And they would
never eat of it unless it were killed in this manner.

Those people go naked, wearing only a piece of cloth made of
palm around their shameful parts. They have as many wives as they
wish, but there is always a chief one. The males, both large and
small, have the head of their member pierced from one side to the
other, with a pin of gold or of tin as thick as a goose feather; and at
each end of this pin some have a star-shaped decoration like a
button, and others, one like the head of a cart nail. Often I wished to
see that of some young men and old men, because I could not believe
it. In the middle of this pin or tube is a hole through which they
urinate, and the pin and the stars always remain firm, holding the
member stiff. They told us that this was the wish of their women,
and that if they did otherwise they would not have intercourse with
them. And when they wish to cohabit with their wives, the latter
themselves take the member without its being prepared or rigid,
and so they put it little by little into their nature, beginning with
the stars. Then when it is inside it stiffens, and remains there until
it becomes soft, for otherwise they would not be able to withdraw
it. And those people do this because they are of a weak nature and
constitution.

Whenever any of our men went ashore and landed, be it by day
or night, everyone invited him to eat and drink. Their viands are
half cooked and very salty. They drink often and much, and their
meal lasts five or six hours. The women loved us very much more
than the men of the country. And all the women, when they are
above the age of ten years, have their nature covered little by little,
because of the men's member made in the aforesaid fashion.

When one of the principal men among them is dead, they practise these ceremonies for him. First, all the ladies of the house go to the dead man's house, where he lies in a coffin. Round this coffin are ropes stretched like lists, to which are attached many branches of trees, and in the middle of each branch is a cotton cloth like a canopy. Beneath this the greatest ladies seat themselves, all veiled and covered with white cotton cloths, each having a maid who fans her with a fan of palm. The other women are seated, all sad and weeping, around the dead man's chamber. Then there is one who with a small knife cuts off little by little the dead man's hair. And there is another (who was the dead man's chief wife) who lays herself upon him, and sets her mouth, her hands and her feet to those of the dead man. And while the other woman is cutting off the hair, the latter one weeps. And when she has ceased cutting, the latter one sings. Within and around the chamber are several porcelain jars with fire, and containing myrrh, storax and benzoin, which strongly scented the chamber. And they keep the dead man five or six days with these ceremonies. And I think that he is anointed with camphor. Then they bury him, in the same coffin or closed box, in a place covered and surrounded by wood.

Every night, in that city, toward the hour of midnight there came a very black bird as large as a crow, and no sooner had it come to the house than it screeched. At which all the dogs howled and bayed. And this screeching and howling lasted five or six hours. And never would they tell us the reason for all this.

CHAPTER XXVII

Excuse of Zzula, lord of Mattan, to the captain. The captain went to Mattan against the lord of Cilapulapu. Fight against those of Mattan. The captain killed. And his eulogy made by the author, Pigafetta.

On Friday the twenty-sixth of April Zzula, lord of the aforesaid island of Mattan, sent one of his sons to present to the captain-general two goats, saying that he would keep all his promises to him, but because of the lord of Cilapulapu (who refused to obey the

King of Spain) he had not been able to send them to him. And he
begged that on the following night he would send but one boat with
some of his men to fight. The captain-general resolved to go there
with three boats. And however strongly we besought him not to
come, yet he (as a good shepherd) would not abandon his sheep. But
at midnight we set forth, sixty men armed with corselets and hel-
mets, together with the Christian king; and we so managed that we
arrived at Mattan three hours before daylight. The captain would
not fight at this hour, but sent by the Moor to tell the lord of the
place and his people that if they agreed to obey the King of Spain,
and recognize the Christian king as their lord, and give us tribute,
they should all be friends. But if they acted otherwise they should
learn by experience how our lances pierced. They replied that they
had lances of bamboo hardened in the fire and stakes dried in the
fire, and that we were to attack them when we would. Then we
waited for day to come, that we might have more men. And that
we said in order to find them in due time. For we had made several
trenches around the houses to make them fall into them.*

When day came, we leapt into the water, being forty-nine men,
and so we went for a distance of two crossbow flights before we
could reach the harbour, and the boats could not come further in-
shore because of the stones and rocks which were in the water. The
other eleven men remained to guard the boats.

Having thus reached land we attacked them. Those people had
formed three divisions, of more than one thousand and fifty persons.†
And immediately they perceived us, they came about us with loud
voices and cries, two divisions on our flanks, and one around and
before us. When the captain saw this he divided us in two and thus
we began to fight. The hackbutmen and crossbowmen fired at long

---

* The Beinecke Ms would appear to be at fault here, and the version in the
Italian Ms is evidently correct: '[They asked us] not to proceed to attack
them at once, but to wait until morning, so that they might have more men.
They said that in order to induce us to go in search of them; for they had dug
certain pitholes between the houses in order that we might fall into them.'
† Between 3,000 and 4,000, according to the Genoese pilot.

range for nearly half an hour, but in vain, [our shafts] merely passing through their shields, made of strips of wood unbound, and their arms. Seeing this, the captain cried out, Do not fire, do not fire any more. But that was of no avail. When those people saw this, and that we fired the hackbuts in vain, they shouted and determined to stand fast. But they shouted louder when the hackbuts were discharged, and then they did not stay still from fear, but jumped hither and thither, covered by their shields. And thus defending themselves they fired at us so many arrows, and lances of bamboo tipped with iron, and pointed stakes hardened by fire, and stones, that we could hardly defend ourselves.

Seeing this the captain sent some of his men to burn the houses of those people in order to frighten them. Who, seeing their houses burning, became bolder and more furious, so that two of our men were killed near these houses, and we burned a good thirty of their houses. Then they came so furiously against us that they sent a poisoned arrow through the captain's leg. Wherefore he ordered us to withdraw slowly, but the men fled while six or eight of us remained with the captain. And those people shot at no other place but our legs, for the latter were bare. Thus for the great number of lances and stones that they threw and discharged at us we could not resist.

Our large pieces of artillery which were in the ships could not help us, because they were firing at too long range, so that we continued to retreat for more than a good crossbow flight from the shore, still fighting, and in water up to our knees. And they followed us, hurling poisoned arrows four or six times; while, recognizing the captain, they turned toward him inasmuch as twice they hurled arrows very close to his head. But as a good captain and a knight he still stood fast with some others, fighting thus for more than an hour. And as he refused to retire further, an Indian threw a bamboo lance in his face, and the captain immediately killed him with his lance, leaving it in his body. Then, trying to lay hand on his sword, he could draw it out but halfway because of a wound from a bamboo lance that he had in his arm. Which seeing, all those people threw themselves on him, and one of them with a large javelin (which is like a partisan, only thicker)* thrust it into his left leg, whereby he fell face downward. On this all at once rushed upon him with lances of iron and of bamboo and with these javelins, so that they slew our mirror, our light, our comfort and our true guide.

While those people were striking him, he several times turned back to see whether we were all at the ships. Then, seeing him dead, as best we could we rescued the wounded men and put them into the boats which were already leaving. The Christian king would have succoured us, but before we landed the captain had ordered and charged him not to leave the ships, but to remain and see in what manner we fought. And the king, knowing that the captain was dead, caused the remainder of our men, both sound and wounded, to withdraw, and we were constrained to leave there the dead body of the captain-general with our other dead.

I hope that, by your most illustrious lordship, the renown of so valiant and noble a captain will not be extinguished or fall into oblivion in our time. For among his other virtues he was more constant in a very high hazard and great affair than ever was any other. He endured hunger better than all the others. He was a navigator and made sea charts. And that that is true was seen openly, for no other had so much natural wit, boldness, or knowledge to sail once round the world, as he had undertaken. This battle was fought on a Saturday, the twenty-seventh day of April, one thousand five hundred and twenty-one. And the captain wished to make it on a Saturday because that was his day of devotion. With him died eight of our men, and four Indians whom we had made Christians. And of the enemy fifteen were killed by the guns of the ships which had finally come to our help; and many of our men were wounded.

---

* The author of this French version has misapprehended the Spanish terms for these two weapons, rendered by him as *javelot* and *partisane* but preserved in the Italian Ms. as *terciado* (cutlass) and *simitara* (scimitar).

CHAPTER XXVIII

The king become Christian requested the captain's body from those of Mattan, who refused it. Commanders elected by the men of the ships. Of their interpreter named Henry, and of his treason. Those of the ships departed, knowing their men to be dead in the island of Zzubu. And of the benefits which came from this.

After dinner the Christian king (with our consent) sent to tell those of Mattan that if they would give us the bodies of the captain and the other dead men, we would give them as much merchandise as they desired. And they answered that they would not give up such a man, as we supposed, and that they would not give him up for the greatest riches in the world, but that they intended to keep him as a perpetual memorial.

As soon as the captain died, the four men of our company, who had remained in the city to trade, had our goods brought to the ships. Then we made and elected two commanders. One was Duarte Barbosa, a Portuguese, and kinsman of the captain;* and the other João Serrão, a Spaniard.† Our interpreter named Henrich (because he had been slightly wounded) no longer went ashore to do our necessary business, but was always wrapped in a blanket. Wherefore Duarte Barbosa, commander of the captain's flagship, told him in a loud voice that, although the captain his master was dead, he would not be set free or released, but that when we reached Spain, he would still be the slave of Madame Beatrix, the wife of the deceased captain-general. And he threatened that if he did not go ashore he would be driven away. The slave, hearing this, rose up and, feigning to take no heed of these words, went on shore and told the Christian king that we were about to depart immediately, but that, if he would follow his advice, he would gain all our ships and merchandise. And so they plotted a conspiracy. Then the slave returned to the ships, and he appeared to behave better‡ than before.

* Brother of Magellan's wife.
† In fact a Portuguese, and brother of Magellan's friend Francisco Serrão.
‡ 'More cunning.' An error by the French translator.

On Wednesday morning the first day of May the Christian king sent to tell the commanders that he had prepared the jewels and presents which he had promised to send to the King of Spain, and that he begged them to go with others of their men to dine with him that morning, and that he would give them all. Then twenty-four men went, and our astrologer named San Martín of Seville. I could not go, because I was all swollen from the wound of a poisoned arrow which I had received in the forehead.

João Carvalho with the constable returned, and told us that they had seen the man who was cured by a miracle leading the priest into his house, and that for this reason they had departed, fearing some evil chance. No sooner had those two spoken their words than we heard great cries and groans. Then we quickly raised the anchors, and firing several pieces of artillery at their houses, we approached nearer to the shore. Firing thus, we perceived João Serrão in his shirt, bound and wounded, who cried out that we should not shoot any more, for we should kill them.★ And we asked him if all the others with the interpreter were dead. And he said that all were dead save the interpreter, and he begged us earnestly to redeem him with some merchandise. But João Carvalho, his friend, and the others would not do so for fear that they would not remain masters if the boat were sent ashore. Then João Serrão, weeping, said that as soon as we sailed he would be killed. And he said that he prayed God that at the day of judgment he would demand his soul of his friend João Carvalho. Thereupon we departed quickly. And I know not whether João Serrão who remained behind be alive or dead.†

In that island are found dogs, cats, rice, millet, ginger, figs, oranges, lemons, sugarcanes, honey, coconuts, sugar, flesh of divers

★ 'For they [the natives] would kill him.' A further error by the French translator.

† The official list gives the names of 27 men massacred, including the Portuguese captains of the three ships (Duarte Barbosa, João Serrão, Luís Affonso de Goes), the pilot Andres de San Martín, and the interpreter Enrique of Malacca.

kinds, palm wine and gold. And it is a large island, with a good port, which has two entrances, one open to the east and northeast, and the other to the west and southwest. It lies in the latitude of ten degrees and eleven minutes toward the Arctic Pole, and in the longitude of one hundred and sixty-four degrees from the line of demarcation. And that island is named Zzubu.

Before the captain died, we had news of the islands of Molucca. Those people play on viols with copper strings.

Some Words of the Aforesaid Heathen Peoples

The man *Lac*	The armpits *Illoc*
The woman *Perampuan*	The arm *Bochen*
The youth *Benibeni*	The elbow *Sico*
The married woman *Babai*	The thumb *Molanghai*
The hair *Boho*	The hand *Camat*
The face *Guay*	The palm *Palan*
The eyelids *Pilac*	The finger *Tudlo*
The eyebrows *Chilei*	The nail *Coco*
The eyes *Matta*	The navel *Pussud*
The nose *Ilon*	The male member *Vtin*
The jaws *Apin*	The genitories *Boto*
The lips *Olol*	The female nature *Billat*
The mouth *Baba*	Intercourse *Iiam*
The teeth *Nepin*	The buttocks *Samput*
The gums *Leghex*	The thighs *Paha*
The tongue *Dilla*	The knee *Tuhud*
The ears *Delenghan*	The leg *Bassabassag*
The throat *Ligh*	The calf of the leg *Bitis*
The neck *Tanghig*	The sole of the foot *Lapalapa*
The chin *Silan*	Gold *Bolaon*
The beard *Bonghot*	Silver *Pilla*
The shoulders *Bagha*	Brass *Concach*
The spine *Lieud*	Iron *Butau*
The breast *Dughan*	Sugarcanes *Tubu*
The body *Tiam*	Rice *Bughaz. Baras*

Honey *Deghes*

Wax *Talo*

Salt *Acin*

Wine *Tuba. Nio. Nipa*

To drink *Minuncubil*

To eat *Macan*

The pig *Babui*

The goat *Candia*

The chicken *Monot*

Millet *Humas*

Pepper *Malissa*

Cloves *Chiande*

Cinnamon *Mana*

Ginger *Luia*

The egg *Itlog*

Vinegar *Zzucha*

Water *Tubin*

Fire *Claio*

Smoke *Assu*

To blow *Tigban*

Balances *Timban*

Weight *Tahil*

The pearl *Muttiara*

Mother-of-pearl *Tipai*

St Job's disease *Alupalan*

Bring me *Palatin comorica*

Good *Maiu*

No *Tida le*

The knife *Cepol sudan*

The scissors *Catle*

To shave *Chuntinch*

A well-adorned man *Pixab*

Cloth *Balandan*

Garments with which they cover themselves *Abaca*

A bell *Colon colon*

Pater Nosters of all sorts *Tacle*

The comb *Cutlei. Missamis*

To comb *Monssugud*

The shirt *Sabun*

The sewing needle *Daghu*

To sew *Mamis*

Porcelain *Moboluc*

The dog *Aiam. Ido*

The cat *Epos*

The veils *Ghapas*

Glass beads *Balus*

Come hither *Marica*

The house *Ilagha. Balai*

The wood *Tatamue*

Mats on which they lie *Taghicā*

Palm mats *Bani*

Cushions of leaves *Vlūnā*

Wooden platters *Dulan*

Their god *Abba*

The sun *Adlo*

The moon *Songhot*

The star *Bolan. Bintun*

The dawn *Mene*

The morning *Vtma*

The evening *Taghai*

Large *Bassal*

The bow *Bossugh*

The arrow *Oghon*

Shields *Calassan*

Their garments in fighting *Baluti*

Their swords *Calix. Baladao*

The spear *Bancau*

The river *Tau*

Fishing nets *Pucat. Laia*

The boat *Sampan*	The ship *Benaoa*
Large canes *Cauaghan*	A king, or a great captain-
Small canes *Boinbon*	general *Raia*
Large boats *Ballāghai*	One *Vzza*
Small boats *Boloto*	Two *Dua*
The fish *Icam. Issida*	Three *Tolo*
Fish all of one colour	Four *Vpat*
Ponapsapan	Five *Lima*
Red fish *Timuan*	Six *Onom*
Another fish *Pilax*	Seven *Pitto*
All fish *Siamasiama*	Eight *Gualu*
A slave *Bonssul*	Nine *Ciam*
The gallows *Bole*	Ten *Polo*

CHAPTER XXIX

The ship Concepción burned. Our men, coasting the island of Panilonghon, came to a large island named Chippit. The honourable reception and friendly treatment which the king of that island gave them. Of the name of the said king. And of the size of the said island.

Eighteen leagues distant from that island of Zzubu, at the head of the other island, which is named Bohol, we burned in the middle of that archipelago the ship Concepción, because there were too few men,* and we supplied the other two ships with the best things that were in her. Then we took a southwesterly course. And about mid-day, [after] coasting the island of Panilonghon† (in which are black men as in Ethiopia), we came to a large island.‡ Its king (to make peace with us) drew blood from his left hand and with it made his body, his face and the end of his tongue bloody, as a mark of the

---

* Of the original complement of about 270 men in the fleet, some 120 only were left to work the ships.
† Panglao, off the southwest coast of Bohol. The ships had sailed southwest through the Bohol Strait. The 'black men' were Negritos.
‡ The northeast part of the island of Mindanao.

greatest friendship. And we did likewise. I went ashore alone with the king to see that island. And no sooner had we entered into a river than some fishermen presented many fish for the king. This done, the king took off the cloth which he had round his privy parts, some of his chief men being with him, and singing he began to row. And, after passing by some places on the river, we came to his house at two hours after nightfall.

From the beginning of the river where our ships were to the king's house was a distance of two leagues. As we entered it, there came to meet us many torches of bamboo and palm leaves, which were of *animes*. While supper was being prepared, the king with two chief men and two of his women, very beautiful, drank up a large jar of palm wine without eating anything. I excused myself, saying that I had supped, and would drink no more than once, and in drinking I observed all the same ceremonies as the King of Mazzaua. Then supper came, which was of rice and fish and very salt broth, all served in porcelain dishes, and they ate rice for bread. And the rice was cooked after this manner. First they put into an earthenware pot (such as we have) a large leaf to line it all round, then they put in water and rice, which they cover, and let it boil until the rice becomes as hard as bread; and afterward they take it out in pieces. Thus they cook the rice in [*sic*] that bread.

After we had supped, the king sent for a reed mat, and another of palm and a pillow of leaves to lie on that night. And the king with his two wives went to sleep in a place apart. When day came, while dinner was in preparation, I walked about that island, where I saw in the king's houses many vessels of gold and little food. Then we dined on rice and fish only. And after dinner I said to the king by signs that I would gladly see the queen. And he replied that he was willing. Then we went, the whole company, to the top of a high mountain, where was the queen's house. Entering it, we bowed to her, and she to me, and then I seated myself beside her. She was making a palm mat to lie on.

In her house were fastened and hanging some porcelain jars, and four bells of metal, one larger than the others, and two smaller ones, for ringing. Many male and female slaves who served her were there. And these houses were made like the others aforesaid. After we had taken our leave, we returned to the king's house, where we were at once given refreshment of sugarcane.

The greatest commodity in that island is abundance of gold. They showed us certain small valleys, making signs to us that there was as much gold there as they had hairs, but that they had no iron nor tools to mine it, and moreover that they would not take the trouble to do so. That part of the island is one and the same land with Butuan and Calaghan, and lies toward Bohol, and borders on Mazzaua. And because we shall return again to that island, I say no more of it.

In the afternoon I wished to return to the ships, and the king and other chief men wished to go thither. And so we went in the same boat. In returning by the river, I perceived to the right, on a small hill, three men hanged from a tree which had its branches cut off. I asked the king what men these were, and he replied that they were malefactors and thieves.

Those people go naked like the others aforesaid. The king is called Raia Calanoa. The port is good. And there are found there rice, ginger, swine, goats, poultry and other things. The island is in the latitude of eight degrees toward the Arctic Pole, and the longitude of one hundred and sixty-six from the line of demarcation, and distant from Zzubu fifty leagues, and it is named Chippit.* And two days from thence is a very large island, called Lozzon,† whither go every year six or eight ships of the peoples named Lechii.‡

* Kipit, east of Sindangan Bay, on the north coast of the Zamboanga Peninsula.
† The earliest European mention of the island of Luzon, the northernmost of the Philippines.
‡ Inhabitants of the Ryukyu Islands ('Lequios'). More probably, Chinese.

CHAPTER XXX

Our men, sailing by other islands whose people are Moors, came to the large island named Pulaoan. Its king made peace with them. And of the produce of that island.

Leaving that place on a course between west and southwest, we came to an island, not very large and almost unihabited, whose people are Moors, and they were banished from an island called Burne.* They go naked like the others. They have bows† with quivers at their side full of arrows poisoned with herbs. They have daggers with hafts enriched with gold and precious stones, lances, bucklers. And they called us holy bodies. In that island little food is found, but plenty of large trees. And it is in latitude seven and a half degrees toward the Arctic Pole, and distant from Chippit forty-three leagues. And it is called Caghaian.‡

About twenty-five leagues from that island, between west and northwest, we discovered a large island, where grow rice, ginger, swine, goats, poultry, figs half a cubit long and as thick as the arm, which are good, and some others much smaller, which are better than all the others. There are also coconuts, sweet potato, sugar-canes, roots like turnips, and rice cooked under the fire in bamboos or wood, which lasts longer than that cooked in pots. We could well call that land the Land of Promise, because before finding it we suffered very great hunger, so that many times we were ready perforce to abandon our ships and go ashore that we might not starve to death. The king of that island made peace with us, making a small cut in his chest with one of our knives, and with his finger marked with blood his tongue and his brow as a sign of truest peace. And we did likewise. That island is in latitude toward the Arctic Pole

---

* Borneo.
† Italian Ms.: *zarobotane* (blowpipes), a word evidently not understood by the French translator.
‡ Cagayan Island, in the group of that name lying in the Sulu Sea west of Mindanao.

nine and a third degrees, and in longitude from the line of demarcation one hundred and sixty and a third. And it is named Pulaoan.*

CHAPTER XXXI

Of the peoples of Palaoan and their bows. Of their cocks. Our men came to a large island, where the king sent them gifts. Of the welcome which he made them. And of what they did in that city. And other things.

The people of Pulaoan go naked like the others, and they all work their fields. They have bows with wooden and tipped arrows longer than a palm, some having long and sharp fishbones poisoned with venomous herbs, and others tipped with poisoned points of bamboo. They have at the head [of the arrow] a piece of soft wood fixed instead of feathers. To the end of their bows† they fasten a piece of iron like [the head of] a mace, with which they fight after shooting all their arrows. They prize brass rings and chains, knives, and even more copper wire for binding their fishhooks. They have very large domestic cocks, which they do not eat for a certain veneration they have for them. Sometimes they make them joust and fight against one another, and each man stakes a wager on his own; then he whose cock is victorious takes the other man's cock and wager. They have wine distilled from rice, stronger and better than that of the palm.

Ten leagues thence to the southwest‡ we came to an island, and as we coasted it, it seemed to me that we went upward. And after we entered the port, the holy body appeared to us in very dark weather. And from the beginning of that island to the port are fifty leagues. The following day, the ninth of July, the king of that island sent us a very fair ship, having the prow and the poop worked in

* Palawan.   † Italian Ms.: 'blowpipes'.

‡ After coasting first northeast and then southwest along Palawan and calling at several villages, they had left its southern point on 21 June 1521, having taken aboard three Moors as pilots. They had passed through the Balabac Strait, between the islands of Balabac and Banggi, and southwest along the coast of Borneo to Brunei.

gold, and at the prow was a white and blue banner with peacock's feathers at the point. Some men played instruments like drums. And with this ship came two *almadies,*★ which are their fishing boats. And this ship was called *prao*, which is like a foist. Then eight old men, among the chief of them, entered the ships and seated themselves on a carpet in the stern, and they presented to us a painted wooden jar full of betel and areca, which are the fruits that they always chew, with orange flowers. The said jar was covered with a cloth of yellow silk. Also they gave us two cages full of poultry, a pair of goats, three jars full of distilled rice wine and some bundles of sugercane. And they did likewise for the other ship. Then they embraced us, and we took leave. The said rice wine is clear as water, but so strong that some of our men became intoxicated, and they call it *arach.*†

Six days later, the king sent again three ships in great pomp, playing instruments and taborins, and they came about our ships and saluted us with their cloth caps, which cover only the top of their head. And we greeted them with our artillery without shot. Then they gave us a present of divers viands all of rice, some wrapped in leaves and made into fairly long pieces, others like sugar loaves, and others made after the manner of tarts with eggs and honey. And they told us that the king was content that we should take water and wood, and should do as we wished. Hearing that, seven of us went aboard the ship and took a present to the king, which was a green velvet robe after the Turkish fashion, a chair of violet velvet, five cubits of red cloth, a red cap, a covered cup, three quires of paper and a gilt writing case. We gave to the queen three cubits of yellow cloth, a pair of silver shoes, and a silver needlecase full of needles. To the governor, three cubits of red cloth, a cap and a gilt cup. To the herald who had come to the ship we gave a robe of red and green cloth after the Turkish fashion, a cap and a quire of paper. And to the seven other chief men, to one a piece of cloth, to others caps, and to each a quire of paper. Then forthwith we departed.

★ Canoes of the East Indies.   † *Araq*, spirituous liquor.

When we arrived at the city, we remained about two hours in the ship until two elephants covered with silk came, and twelve men, each with a porcelain jar covered with silk, to carry our gifts. Then we mounted the elephants, and the twelve men marched ahead with the jars and gifts. And so we went to the governor's house, where we were given a supper of divers viands, and at night we slept on cotton mattresses. Next day we remained in the house until noon. Then we went to the king's palace on the said elephants, with the gifts ahead, as on the previous day. Between the house and the king's palace all the streets were full of people with swords, spears and targets, for the king had willed it thus. And we entered the palace courtyard on the elephants. Then we mounted by steps, accompanied by the governor and other notables. And we entered a large hall full of barons and lords, where we were seated on a carpet with the gifts and vessels with us.

At the head and end of this hall was another one, higher but not so large, and all hung with silk drapery, and from it two windows with crimson curtains opened, by which light entered the hall. Three hundred naked men were standing there with swords and sharp stakes posed at their thigh to guard the king. And at the end of this hall was a window, and when a crimson curtain was drawn, we perceived within the king seated at a table, with one of his little sons, and they were chewing betel. Behind him were only many ladies. Then one of the chief men told us that we could not speak to the king, but that if we desired anything we should tell him, and he would tell a more notable man, who would communicate it to one of the governor's brothers, who was in the smaller hall, and he would speak through a speaking tube by a hole in the wall to the one who was inside with the king. And he instructed us that we were to make three obeisances to the king with hands clasped above our head, raising our feet one after the other since we had to kiss them.

All this was done, after the manner of their royal obeisance. And we told him that we were servants of the King of Spain, who desired peace with him and required no more than to do trade. The king caused us to be told that since the King of Spain was his friend, he was very willing to be his, and he ordered that we should be allowed to take water and wood and merchandise at our will. This done, we gave him presents, to which at each thing he made a little bow with his head. Then on his behalf were given to each of us cloths of crimson and gold and silk, which they put on our left shoulders. And they forthwith gave us a collation of cloves and cinnamon. Then the curtains were quickly drawn and the windows closed. All the men in the palace had cloth of gold and of silk round their shameful parts, daggers with gold handles, adorned with pearls and precious stones, and many rings on their fingers.

After this we returned on the elephants to the governor's house, whither seven men carried the king's gift ahead. And when we arrived there, they gave to each of us his gift, and they put it on our left shoulders, in return for which we gave each of them for their trouble a pair of knives. While we were at the governor's house, nine men came from the king with as many very large wooden trays, and in each tray were ten or twelve porcelain plates filled with flesh of calf, capons, chickens, peacocks and other animals, with fish. And we supped there on the ground (on a palm mat) from thirty-two kinds of meat, besides the fish and other things, and at each mouthful we drank from a porcelain cup as big as an egg the aforesaid distilled wine. We ate rice and other sweetmeats with golden spoons, after our fashion. Where we slept two nights, there were two torches of white wax burning in two rather tall silver candlesticks, and two large lamps filled with oil, each having four wicks, and two men were continually snuffing them. After that we went on the elephants to the seashore, where two of their boats were ready and took us to our ships.

That city* is all built in salt water, except the king's house, and the houses of certain chief men. And it has twenty or twenty-five thousand hearths. All their houses are of wood, and built on great beams raised from the ground. And when the tide is high, the women go ashore in boats to sell and buy the things necessary for their food. In front of the king's house is a thick wall of brick, with

* Brunei.

towers in the manner of a fortress, and in it were fifty-six large brass cannon, and six of iron. And in the two days that we were there they discharged many of them.

That king is a Moor, and he is named Raia Siripada, and aged forty years. He was fat, and no one rules him except the ladies and daughters of the chief men. He never leaves his palace save when he goes hunting. And one cannot speak to him but through a speaking tube. He keeps two scribes who write down all his state and business on very thin tree bark. And they are called *Xiritoles*.

CHAPTER XXXII

Our men took several Prao and Junces and killed many of their men. And they took the son of the king of the island of Lozzon, whom the pilot let go. Of the Moorish king. People of the said king held by our men. Of junces. Of porcelain. The price of merchandise. Of the two pearls of the King of Burne. The law of the Moors. Of camphor and other things.

On Monday morning the twenty-ninth of July, we saw coming toward us more than a hundred of those ships, called *prao*, divided into three squadrons, with as many other *tunghuli*, which are their small boats. Seeing this, and suspecting some deceit and treason, we made sail as quickly as possible. And for greater haste we slipped one anchor, and we had great fear of being surprised in the middle of certain ships called *junces* [junks], which the day before anchored after us. We quickly turned upon them, and took four, killing many men, and three or four of those junks took flight and ran aground. In one of those which we took was the son of the king of the island of Lozzon, who was captain-general of the King of Burne, and he came with these junks from a large town called Laoe,★ which is at the head of this island toward Java Major. And he had destroyed and sacked that town for refusing to obey that king, but [instead] the King of Java Major.

João Carvalho, our pilot, allowed this captain and the junk to go

★ Perhaps the island of Laut, off the southeast coast of Borneo.

without our consent in return for a quantity of gold (as we learned later). And if he had not let him go, the king would have given us all that we demanded, since that captain was highly esteemed in those parts, but more by the heathen because they are great enemies of that Moorish king.

In that port is another city of heathen, larger than that of the Moors, also built on salt water. Wherefore every day those two peoples fight in the same port. The heathen king is as powerful as the Moorish king, but not so proud, and he might easily be converted to the faith of Jesus Christ. When the Moorish king heard in what manner we had treated the junks, he sent to tell us by one of our men who were ashore that the aforesaid ships called *Prao* had not come to do us harm, but were going against the heathen. And in proof of this they showed some heads of dead men, saying that they were heathen. Then we sent to him to ask that he be pleased to allow two of our men to come, who were in the city on some business, and the son of João Carvalho who had been born in the land of Verzin. And the king refused. And the cause of this was Carvalho himself, for letting the said captain go. Wherefore we held sixteen of the most notable men, to bring them back to Spain, and three ladies in the name of the Queen of Spain. But João Carvalho took them for himself.

Those junks which are the ships of those people are made in this manner. The hull stands about two palms high in the water, and is of large planks fastened with wooden pegs, very well made, and they are covered over all with bamboos. And one of those junks carries as much cargo as a ship. On each side are very thick bamboos as a counterweight. Their masts are of bamboo, and the sails of the bark of trees.

Porcelain is a kind of very white earthenware, and is fifty years underground before being worked, for otherwise it would not be fine. And the father buries it for the son. And if poison or venom is put into a fine porcelain jar, it will immediately break. The money coined by the Moors in those parts is of metal, pierced in the centre for stringing. And it bears only, on one side, four marks, which are letters of the great king of China, and they call it *picis*. For a *cathil* of quicksilver (which makes two of our pounds) they gave us six porcelain dishes. For a *cathil* of metal, a porcelain vase. For three knives, as much. For a quire of paper, a hundred *picis*. For six hundred *cathils* of metal, they gave us a cask★ of wax, worth two hundred and three *cathils*. For four hundred *cathils* of metal, a cask of salt. For forty *cathils* of metal, a cask of pitch for the ship, for there is none in those places. Twenty *tahili* make one *cathil*. They hold in great esteem quicksilver, glass, linen, cloth, and all our other goods, but even more, iron and spectacles. Those Moors go naked like the others. They drink quicksilver. The sick man drinks it as a medicine to purge himself, and the healthy man to keep his health.

The King of Burne has two pearls as large as two eggs, and they are so round that they cannot lie still on a table. And of this I am certain. For when we bore the gifts to him, signs were made to him that he should show them to us, and he replied that he would do so on the morrow. And this he did.

The Moors worship Mahomet, and their law is not to eat the flesh of swine, nor to wash their backside with the left hand, nor to eat with it,† nor to cut up and slice anything with the right hand, nor to sit down when they urinate, nor to kill poultry or goats unless they have first addressed the sun, to cut off the wing tips of poultry and the small pieces of skin growing under them and then to split them down the middle, to wash their face with the right hand, not to wash their teeth with the fingers, and to eat nothing killed unless by them. And they are circumcised like Jews.

In that island is produced camphor, a kind of balsam, which grows between the wood and the bark of the tree, and is small, and if it is exposed it disappears little by little, and they call it *capor*. There also are produced cinnamon, ginger, myrobalans, oranges, lemons, capers, melons, cucumbers, sugar, onions, cows, oxen, pigs, goats, poultry, geese, stags, hinds, elephants, horses and many

★ In the Italian Ms., *bahar*, a weight used in Calicut.
† The French text makes nonsense of this sentence, which in the Italian Ms. reads: 'as they wash the backside with the left hand, not to eat with that hand.'

other things. This island is so large that it would take three months to sail round it in a *prao*. It is in the latitude of five and a quarter degrees toward the Arctic Pole, and the longitude of one hundred and seventy-six and two thirds degrees from the line of demarcation. And it is named Burne.

CHAPTER XXXIII

Our people repair the ships. As they sailed they took a prao. Of the wild boars which they found in an island, crocodiles, and a strange fish. Of the living leaves. The Governor of Pulaoan taken. Of the islands of Zzolo and Taghima where large pearls grow. Of the island of Monoripa where cinnamon grows. And of the cinnamon tree.

Leaving that island we turned back* to find a convenient place to repair our ships, because one of them was taking water. The pilot not paying heed, she had struck on some rocks of an island named Bibalon,† but with the help of God we saved her. And then pursuing our course we took a *prao* loaded with coconuts, which was going to Burne, and the men in her fled to a little island, until we had taken the fruit. And three other *prao* fled behind certain other small islands.

At the cape of Burne (between that island and another called Cimbombom,‡ which is in eight degrees and seven minutes) is a port meet for repairing ships, which we entered. And because we lacked many things necessary for the repair of the ships we remained there forty-two days.§ In this time each of us was occupied, and we laboured some at one thing, some at another. But the greatest labour which we had was that of searching for and cutting wood in the forests, without shoes.

In that island are wild boars, one of which we killed in the water,

---

* That is, northeast along the Borneo coast.
† A name recorded only by Pigafetta. Presumably a reef between the Balabac Strait and Brunei.
‡ Cape Sempang Mangayau, the northernmost point of Borneo.
§ 15 August–27 September 1521.

as we passed in the boat from one island to another. Its head was two and a half feet long, with large teeth. There are large crocodiles both in the sea and on land, oysters and shellfish of divers kinds. Among others we found two, of which the flesh of one weighed twenty-five pounds, and of the other forty-four pounds. We caught a fish which had a head like a pig's with two horns, and the body was all of a single bone, and it had a kind of saddle on its spine, and it was small. Also trees are found there making leaves which, when they fall, are alive and walk.* And these leaves are no larger or smaller than those of a mulberry, but not so long. Near the tail, which is short and pointed, they have on both sides two feet. They have no blood, and if anyone touches them they run away. I kept one for nine days in a cage, and when I opened it it went all around. They cannot, as I think, live on anything but air.

Having left that port,† at the cape of the island of Pulaoan‡ we encountered a junk coming from Burne, in which was the Governor of Pulaoan, to which we signalled that it should lower its sails. As they refused to do this, we took them by force and pillaged it. And the governor, for his release, promised to give us within seven days four hundred measures of rice, twenty pigs, twenty goats and a hundred and fifty chickens. Then he presented to us coconuts, figs, sugarcanes, jars of palm wine and other things. Seeing his liberality, we returned to him some of his daggers and arquebuses and we gave a banner, a robe of yellow damask and five cubits of cloth to him; and to one of his sons, a cloak of blue cloth; and to the governor's brother, a robe of green cloth and other things. And we parted from him as friends.

Then we turned back between the island of Caghaian and the port of Chippit, laying course east by southeast, to find the islands of Molucca, and we passed by certain small hills,§ toward which we

---

* These were insects resembling leaves.

† On 27 September. João Carvalho was on this day removed from command, becoming again chief pilot; Espinosa was appointed captain of *Trinidad*, and Elcano captain of *Victoria*.

‡ Cape Buliluyan, the southernmost point of Palawan.   § *i.e.* coral reefs.

found the sea full of weed and very deep. And when we were passing by those little hills, we seemed to be entering another sea. Leaving Chippit to the east, we discovered two islands, Zzolo and Taghima,★ to the west, near which grow pearls, and the two large pearls aforesaid of the King of Burne were found there, and he had them (as we were told) in this manner. That king took for wife a daughter of the King of Zzolo, who told him that her father had these two pearls. Hearing this, the king deliberated how to obtain them in whatever manner might be. Wherefore he went one night with fifty *prao*, and took the said king and two of his sons, whom he carried off to Burne. And he told the King of Zzolo that for his ransom he should give him the two pearls.

Sailing east by northeast we passed between the settlements called Cavit and Subanin, and an inhabited island named Monoripa,† ten leagues distant from the aforesaid hillocks. And the people of that island have their houses on boats, and dwell nowhere else. These two settlements of Cavit and Subanin (which are in the islands of Butuan and Calagan) produce the best cinnamon that can be found. And we remained there two days, and loaded our ships with it. But in order to have a good wind for passing a cape and some small islands which lay about it, we were unwilling to stay longer, and making sail we exchanged and received seventeen pounds of cinnamon for two of the large knives which we had taken from the governor of Pulaoan. This cinnamon tree is no taller than three or four cubits, and as thick as the finger of a hand, and it has no more than three or four branches, and its leaf is like that of the laurel, and its bark is the cinnamon, which is gathered twice a year. So the wood grows strongly and the leaves when green smell like the cinnamon. And they call it *caiumana*. *Caiu* means wood and *mana* sweet, hence sweet wood.

★ Jolo and Basilan, in the Sulu Archipelago.
† Cavite and Subanin are on the west coast of the Zamboanga Peninsula, Mindanao. The ships then sailed through Basilan Strait, in which *Monoripa* (perhaps the island of Sacol) is to be sought, into Moro Gulf, and eastward across it.

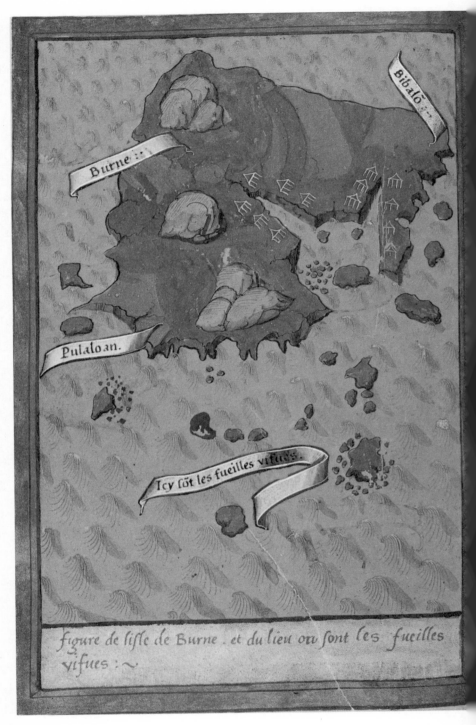

Bibalõ

Burne

Pulalo an.

Icy sõt les fueilles vifues.

figure de lisle de Burne. et du lieu ou sont les fueilles vifues :~

The Island of Burne, and of the place where the living leaves are.

CHAPTER XXXIV

Our people took by force a ship called binidai, in which the brother of the King of Maingdanao gave them news of Molucca. And of the men of Butuan and Calagan.

Laying course to the northeast, and going to a great city named Maingdanao* (which is in the island of Butuan and Calagan), that we might have some information about Molucca, we took by force a ship termed *binidai*,† which is like a *prao*, and in which we killed seven men. There were only seventeen men, as bold and ready as any others whom we had seen in those parts, and all chiefs of Maingdanao. One of them told us that he was a brother of the King of the said Maingdanao, and that he knew well where Molucca was. On which we left our northeast course and took that to southeast. On a headland of this island of Butuan and Calagan, near a river, are hairy men, very great fighters and good archers, who have swords a palm in length. For the most part they eat nothing but the raw hearts of men with the juice of oranges or lemons, and these hairy men are called Benaian.‡ When we took the southeast course, we lay in the latitude of six degrees and seven minutes toward the Arctic Pole and twenty leagues from Cavit.

---

* Magindanau, the principal Malay settlement in the southern port of the island of Mindanao, lay in the delta of the Pulangi River.

† Perhaps a boat resembling a large banca.

‡ Cape Benuian is in northern Mindanao.

CHAPTER XXXV

*Our people in danger and peril saw the three saints, St Elmo, St Nicholas, and
St Clara. And passing by a port they took by force two pilots to show them the
way to Molucca. The brother of the King of Maingdanao escaped, and his
son was drowned. Then they sailed by several small islands.*

Going to the southeast, we found four islands, to wit Ciboque,
Birahanbatluch, Toluch, Saranghani, and Candinghar.* And on
a Saturday by night, the twenty-sixth day of October, coasting
Birahanbatluch, a great storm assailed us. Wherefore, praying to
God, we struck all the sails, and immediately our three saints
appeared, dispelling all the darkness, namely St Elmo, St Nicholas,
and St Clara. St Elmo remained more than two hours at the maintop, like a torch; St Nicholas at the mizzentop; and St Clara at the
foretop. Then we promised each of them a slave and made our alms
to them. Pursuing our way we entered a port between the two
islands of Saranghani and Candinghar, and we anchored to the east
near a settlement of Saranghani, where gold and pearls are found.
Those people are heathen, and they go naked like the others.

This port is in five degrees and nine minutes' latitude, and fifty
leagues distant from Cavit. While there we one day took two pilots
by force that we might learn from them of Molucca. And setting
our course between south and southwest we passed by eight
islands, inhabited and uninhabited, lying in the manner of a street
and named Cheava, Caviao, Cabiao, Camanuzza, Cabaluzzar, Cheai,
Lipan and Nuzza.† Finally we came to an island situated at the
extremity of the said islands, which was very beautiful to behold.
And it happened that we had a contrary wind, and not being able to

* Ciboque is perhaps Sibago off the northeast coast of the large island of Basilan;
Birahanbatluch and Saranghani, the district of Batulaki, on the mainland of
Mindanao, and the island of Sarangani in the group named after the latter,
south of Mindanao; Cardinghar probably represents the island of Balut.
† Islands of the Kawio and Sangihe archipelagos, extending southward from
Mindanao to Celebes. The second and third may be identified phonetically
as Kawio; the fifth as Kawalusu; and the seventh as Lipang.

round a point of that island we sailed hither and thither about it. Wherefore one of the men whom we had taken at Saranghani and the brother of the King of Maingdanao with his little son escaped during the night by swimming to that island. But the son was drowned because he could not keep a firm hold on his father's shoulders. Not being able to raise the said point or cape, we passed below an island where there were many small islands. This island is held by four kings: the Kings Raia Matandatu, Raia Lalagha, Raia Bapti, and Raia Parabu. And they are heathen. This island is in three and a half degrees to the Arctic Pole, and twenty-seven leagues distant from Saranghani, and it is called Sanghir.*

CHAPTER XXXVI

Of the six islands by which our people passed. Of their names, and of their kings. And of the joy which our men had when they perceived the islands of Molucca.

Keeping the same course, we passed about six islands, named Cheama, Carachita, Para, Zzangalura.† Ciau‡ is ten leagues distant from Sanghir, and has a high but not broad mountain, and the king is named Raia Ponto. And Paghinzara,§ at eight leagues from Ciau, has three high mountains, and its king is called Raia Babintau. All these islands are inhabited by heathen. To the east of Cheama is an island called Talaut.‖ Then, to the east of Paghinzara and twelve leagues distant from it, we found two islands, not very large, and inhabited, named Zzoar and Meau.¶ Having passed

* Sangihe, the largest island of the Sangihe group, to the north of Celebes.
† Islands of the Sangihe Archipelago, extending southward toward the north point of Celebes; identifiable, from their orthography, as Kima, Karakitang, Para, Sanggeluhang.   ‡ Siau.
§ Tahulandang, Ruang, or Biaro; the southernmost islands of the Sangihe group.
‖ This parenthetical reference, perhaps displaced, seems to be to the Talaud Islands.
¶ Tifore and Maju, in the Molucca Passage.

these two islands, on Wednesday the sixth of November we discovered four high islands to the east,* fourteen leagues from the two islands. On this the pilot who had remained with us said that these four islands were Molucca. Wherefore we gave thanks to God, and for our great joy we discharged all our artillery. It is no wonder that we should be so joyful, for we had suffered travail and perils for the space of twenty-five months less two days in the search for Molucca. And among all those islands even to Molucca the shallowest bottom that we found was of one hundred and two hundred fathoms, quite to the contrary of what the Portuguese had told us, that you could not navigate there because of the great shoals and the darkness of the sky (as they thought), in which they were deceived.

On Friday the eighth of November, one thousand five hundred and twenty-one, three hours before the setting of the sun, we entered the port of an island called Tadore,† and after anchoring in a depth of twenty fathoms we discharged all our artillery. And the next day the king came in a *prao* to our ships, circling them once, and we immediately went to meet him in a boat to do him honour. And he made us enter his *prao* and sit beside him. He was seated beneath a canopy of silk which gave him shade all round, and before him stood one of his sons with the royal sceptre, and two men bearing golden vessels for washing of his hands, and two other men holding golden vessels full of betel.

The king told us that we were welcome, and related how long ago he had dreamed that ships were coming from distant and strange [parts] to Molucca, and that to have assurance of this he observed the moon by astrology, whereby he saw that we were coming, and knew that we were they. Then the king entered our ships, where we all kissed his hand, and then we led him up to the poop, and there we set him on a chair of red velvet, and clad him in a robe of turquoise-yellow velvet. And to do him more honour each of us sat on the ground beside him. When we were all seated, the king began to say that he and all his peoples desired always to be true friends

* Ternate, Tidore, and adjacent islands of the Moluccas.   † Tidore.

and very loyal vassals of our King of Spain, and that he received us kindly as his children, and that we were assuredly to abide there as in our own houses, for that from this time his island would not no longer be named Tadore but Castille, for the great love that he bore to the king our lord.

We gave him as gifts the aforesaid robe and chair, a piece of fine linen, four cubits of scarlet cloth, a crimson satin, a piece of yellow damask, some Indian cloths worked with gold and silk, a piece of white cloth which is linen of Cambay, two caps, six crystal glasses, twelve knives, three large mirrors, seven pairs of scissors, six combs and many other things. To his son we presented an Indian cloth worked with gold and silk, a large mirror, a cap and two knives. To nine others of his chief men we gave to each a silk cloth, two caps and two knives; and to several others we gave silk cloths to some, knives to others, and caps to others, so that at length the king told us that it was enough. And then he said that he had nothing else to send to his lord the King of Spain except his life, and that we were to approach nearer to the city, and that if anyone should come by night to the ships we should kill him with our hackbuts. After all this the king, having taken leave of us, departed, and at his departure we discharged all our artillery. This king is a Moor and aged fifty-five years, well proportioned with a royal presence and eloquence, and a great astrologer. He was then clad in a white shirt of very fine linen with the top of the sleeves worked with gold, and he had a white cloth from his waist almost to the ground, and he was unshod, and had round his head a silk veil with, above it, a crown of flowers. And he was named Raia Sultan Manzor.

On Sunday the tenth of November, this king desired to know how long it was since we left Spain, and what pay the king gave to each of us, and he desired that we should give him a signature of the king and a royal banner, for that henceforth he had determined that his island and another called Tarenate* (of which his nephew,†

* Ternate, the northernmost of the Moluccas, whose sultan had been murdered eight months earlier.
† Evidently a mistake by the French translator. The Italian Ms. has grandson.

named Colanoghapi, might be crowned king) should both be held
of the King of Castille, and for the honour of his king he was ready
to fight to the death, and when he could no longer resist and defend
himself, he would go to Spain, he and all his people, in a junk.
Thereon he begged us to leave him some of our men, that he might
always have a better reminder of the King of Spain, and not merchandise which would not remain to him. And because he had not
enough merchandise to supply our ships, he told us that he would
go to an island called Bacchian,* the better and more quickly to
supply our ships with cloves, for that he had not enough dry cloves
in his island to load two ships. On that day (since it was Sunday)
we did not wish to do any trade, and the day when they made
festival is Friday.

That your most illustrious lordship may know the islands where
the cloves grow, there are five of them, namely Tarenate, Tadore,
Mutir, Machian and Bacchian.† Tarenate is the first and principal
one. And when its king was alive he was master of nearly all the
others. Tadore is the island where we were, which has its king as
we have said. Mutir and Machian have no king, but are ruled by the
people. And when the two kings of Tarenate and Tadore make war
together these two islands furnish them with men. The other island
is Bacchian, which has a king. All that province where the cloves
grow is named Molucca.

It was not yet eight months since a Portuguese called Francisco
Serrão, captain-general of the king of Tarenate against the King of
Tadore, had died in Tarenate.‡ And he did so much that he constrained the King of Tadore to bestow one of his daughters as wife
on the said King of Tarenate, and to give almost all the children of
his chief men as hostages. Of this daughter was born that nephew

* Batjan, the largest and southernmost island of the Moluccas.
† Ternate, Tidore, Motir, Makian, Batjan.
‡ Francisco Serrão had commanded one of the three ships in the squadron of
António de Abreu, which sailed from Malacca in December 1511 for the dis-
covery of the Moluccas and visited Bali, Sumbawa, Amboina, and Ceram
before turning back.

of the King of Tadore. Then was peace made between them. One day, Francisco Serrão being come to Tadore to buy cloves, this king had him poisoned with leaves of the said betel, and he lived but four days. His king wished to have him buried according to his manners and rites, but three Christians who were his servants would not consent to it. This Francisco left a son and a small daughter, whom he had by a woman whom he took in Java the Great, and two hundred barrels of cloves. He was a great friend and a relative of our good and loyal dead captain-general,* and was the cause for moving him to make this enterprise and voyage, because he had several times, when our captain was at Malacca, written to tell him that he was there.

Since Dom Manuel, then King of Portugal, refused to increase the pensions and pay of our said captain-general by more than one testoon a month in spite of all his feats and merits, he came to Spain where he received from his Sacred Majesty all that he would ask. Ten days after the death of Francisco Serrão, the King of Tarenate, named Raia Abuleis, having driven out his son-in-law the King of Bacchian, was poisoned by his daughter, the wife of the said king, under pretext of wishing to conclude peace between them; and he lived only two days, and left nine principal sons named Clechily momoli, Tadore unughi, Checchily de roix, Cili manzur, Cili paggi, Chialin checchilin, Catara, Vaiechuserich, and Colano ghappi.

* Serrão's relationship to Magellan is unknown.

CHAPTER XXXVII

The son of the King of Tarenate came to the ships. Of Pedro Afonso de Lorosa a Portuguese. Of the wives of the kings of those countries. Of the King of Tadore. Of the heathen peoples. The king caused a house to be built for our men's merchandise. The manner of trading. And of the water with which our men supplied their ships.

On Monday the eleventh of November one of the sons of the King of Tarenate, Checchily de roix, came to our ships clad in red velvet, with two *prao*, beating drums of brass, and would not enter our ships at that time. He had the wife, the children, and all the other goods of the said Francisco Serrão. When we recognized him we sent to ask the king if we should receive him, since we were in his port. And the king replied that we should do as we wished. This son of the king, seeing that we were hesitant and in doubt about him, withdrew a little from our ships, and we went to him with one boat. And we gave him an Indian cloth of gold and of silk, knives, mirrors and scissors, which he took with a somewhat ill grace and immediately departed.

This son had with him a Christian Indian called Manuel, the servant of a Portuguese named Pedro Afonso de Lorosa, who had come from Bandan to Tarenate after the death of Francisco Serrão. And this servant, because he could speak Portuguese, came on board our ships and told us that, although the sons of the King of Tarenate were enemies of the King of Tadore, they were nevertheless always at the service of the King of Spain. Hearing this, we sent a letter to the said Pedro Afonso de Lorosa by this servant of his, and we wrote saying that he should come boldly to us.

Those kings have as many wives as they wish, but they have one principal wife whom all the others obey. The King of Tadore had a large house outside the city, where he kept two hundred of his chief women, with as many others who serve them. When the king eats, he is quite alone, or with his principal wife, in a high place like a gallery, whence he can see all the others who are seated around, and to the one who pleases him most he sends word that she shall come to sleep with him that night. And after his dinner, if he commands that these women eat together, they do so; if not, each of them retires and goes to eat in her own chamber. And no one may see them without the leave and permission of the king. And if anyone is found by day or by night near the king's house, he is killed. Each family and household is obliged to give to the king one or two daughters. And this king had twenty-six children, eight of them sons and the rest daughters.

Before this island is another very large one named Giailolo,* inhabited by Moors and heathen. And there were (as the king told us) two kings among the Moors, one of whom had had six hundred children, and the other five hundred and twenty-five. The heathen do not keep so many wives, and do not live so superstitiously as the Moors; but in the morning, as they leave their house, they worship the first thing that they see for the whole day. The king of those heathens, called Raia Papua, is very rich in gold and lives in the interior of the island. In that island of Giailolo there grow on rocks and stones reeds† as thick as the leg, full of water very good to drink, of which we purchased much.

On Tuesday the twelfth of November, the king caused a house to be constructed in one day to take our merchandise, and we carried almost all of it thither. And to guard it we left three of our men. Then forthwith we began to trade in this manner. For two cubits of fairly good red cloth, we were given a *bahar* of cloves, which contains four quintals and six pounds, and a quintal is worth a hundred pounds. For fifteen cubits or pieces of not very good cloth, one *bahar*. For fifteen axes, one *bahar*. For thirty-five glasses, one *bahar*. And the king had all that. For seventeen *cathils* of cinnabar,‡ one *bahar*. For seventeen *cathils* of quicksilver, one *bahar*. For twenty-five pieces of linen, one *bahar*. For twenty-four of finer quality, one *bahar*. For one hundred and fifty knives, one *bahar*. For fifty pairs of

---

* Halmahera (Gilolo).   † Presumably bamboos.
‡ *Cathil*, a Chinese weight equivalent to about 1¼ pounds. Cinnabar, red sulfide of mercury.

scissors, one *bahar*. For forty caps, one *bahar*. For ten ells of Gujarat cloth, one *bahar*. For a quintal of bronze, one *bahar*. All the mirrors were broken, but the king wished to have all the small good ones.

Many of these things were from the aforesaid junks that we had taken, and our urgent desire to return to Spain made us trade our goods more cheaply than we should otherwise have done. Every day there came to our ships so many boats full of poultry, goats, pigs, coconuts and other things to eat that it was a marvel to see. Then we supplied our ships with good water, which comes from warm earth, but if it is for a space of two hours away from its spring, it quickly becomes cold. This is the contrary of what they said in Spain, that water was brought from a distant country to Molucca.★

CHAPTER XXXVIII

Our men gave to the King of Tadore the captive Indians. Inquiry made by the king of the Portuguese Pedro Afonso. His reply on the discovery of the islands of Molucca. The said king went in search of cloves. The Moorish King of Giailolo came to the ships, and he desired to see the artillery fired.

On Wednesday the king sent his son, named Mossohap a Mutir, that we might be more quickly supplied with cloves. And that very day we told the king that we had taken some Indians. When he heard this he gave thanks to God, and begged us to do him the favour of giving him the prisoners, whom he would send throughout his country with five of his men to publish the fame of the King of Spain. Then we gave him the three women captives, in the name of the queen, for this cause. And next day we presented to him all the prisoners, except those of Burne, and the king took great pleasure in this. Then he begged us, for love of him, to kill all the pigs which we had in our ships, for which he would give us as many goats and poultry, and to hang the dead pigs in a covered and enclosed place, so that, if perchance his people saw them, they should cover

★ Probably it was because of this belief that the ships intended to take in water near Celebes.

their faces in order not to see them or smell their odour. And we did this to give him pleasure.

In the evening of the same day Pedro Afonso the Portuguese* came in a *prao*, and before he had landed from it the king sent to seek him, and laughing he told him that, even though he was by residence of Tarenate, he should speak the truth in reply to all our questions. Then he [Pedro Afonso] told us that he had already been sixteen years in India, and ten in Molucca, and that it was as many years since Molucca had been secretly discovered, and that one year less fifteen days ago a great ship of Malacca had come there and left with a cargo of cloves. But by reason of bad weather she remained at Bandan some months, and her captain was Tristão de Meneses, a Portuguese. And he [Pedro Afonso] had asked him what news there was in Christendom; and he had replied that a fleet of five ships had sailed from Seville to discover Molucca in the name of the King of Spain, with Fernão de Magalhães a Portuguese as captain. And that the King of Portugal, in anger that a Portuguese should oppose him, had sent some ships to the Cape of Good Hope, and as many to Cape St Mary† where the cannibals lived, to guard and forbid the passage, and that he had not found them.

Then the King of Portugal was informed that the said captain had passed by another sea and was going to Molucca, whereupon he wrote immediately to his great captain of India, named Diogo Lopes de Sequeira,‡ that he should send six ships to Molucca. But this Diogo did not send them because of the Grand Turk who was coming to Malacca, which compelled him to send sixty sail to the Strait of Mecca in the land of Judah.§ And they found nothing but a few galleys beached on the shore of that strong and beautiful town of Aden, all of which they burned. After this Diogo sent against us at Molucca a great galleon with two ships of artillery‖ but because

---

* Pedro Afonso de Lorosa, who had come to the Moluccas with Francisco Serrão in 1512.   † At the mouth of the Rio de la Plata.
‡ Diogo Lopes de Sequeira was captain-general of India 1518–22.
§ Jiddah, on the Red Sea, the port of Mecca.
‖ The Italian Ms. reads: 'with two tiers of guns'.

of large stones and rocks, and the currents that flow about Malacca, and contrary winds, they could not pass and turned back. The captain of this galleon was Francisco Faria, a Portuguese.* Then he related to us that a few days earlier a caravel with two junks had been there to learn news of us. But the junks went to Bacchian to load cloves with seven Portuguese. And because they did not respect the king's wives and subjects, although the king often told them and desired them not to behave thus, they, refusing to abstain and withdraw, were killed. And when the men of the caravel learned this, they immediately returned to Malacca, leaving the junks with four hundred *bahar* of cloves and as much merchandise as would purchase another hundred *bahar*. Moreover he told us that every year many junks come from Malacca to Bandan to take and load mace and nutmeg, and from Bandan to Molucca to get cloves. And that these people go with their junks from Molucca to Bandan in three days, and from Bandan to Malacca in fifteen. And that the King of Portugal had already secretly enjoyed Molucca for ten years, that the King of Spain should not know. This Pedro Afonso remained with us until three o'clock of the night, and he told us many other things, and we so dealt with him (promising him good wages and salaries) that he promised to come with us to Spain.†

On Friday the fifteenth of November, the king told us that he was going to Bacchian to fetch the said cloves that those Portuguese had left there, and he requested of us two presents to give to the two governors of Mutir in the name of the King of Spain. And passing through our ships he wished to see how we fired our hackbuts, crossbows and culverins, which are larger than an arquebus, and the king fired three shots of a crossbow, for that pleased him more than the other weapons.

On Sunday the Moorish King of Giailolo came to our ships with

* Probably Pedro de Faria.
† Pedro Afonso did in fact sail with the ships in December 1521, but never reached Spain. He was in the *Trinidad* when she was captured by the Portuguese squadron under António de Brito at Ternate in May 1522, and executed as a traitor

several *prao*, and we gave him a green damask silk, two cubits of red cloth, mirrors, scissors, knives, combs and two gilt glasses. And he said that, since we were friends of the King of Tadore, we were also his, because he loved him like his own son, and if ever any of us went into his country he would do him very great honour. This king was very old, and feared through all those islands for the great power that he had; and he was named Raia Iussu. And this island of Giailolo is so large that one takes four months to sail round it in a prao. On Sunday morning this same king came to the ships, and he wished to see in what manner we fought, and how we fired and discharged our artillery, taking very great pleasure in it; and then he suddenly departed. And (as we were told) this king had in his youth been a great warrior.

CHAPTER XXXIX

Of the tree that bears cloves. The season for harvesting them. Of the tree that bears nutmegs. Of cloths from the bark of trees. Of palm bread. Of the coming of the King of Tadore. Of the suspicion which our men had for the said king. His remonstrance. Of the oath of fidelity that he gave them. And the faith that our men promised him.

On that day of Sunday I went ashore to see how the cloves grow. The tree is tall and as thick across as a man. Its branches in the centre spread out widely, but at the top they grow into a kind of peak. The leaf is like that of a laurel, and the bark of the colour of brown tan. The cloves come at the tip of branches, ten or twenty together. These trees almost always bear more of them on one side than on the other, according to the season. When the cloves sprout, they are white; when ripe, red; and when dried, black. They gather them twice a year, once at Christmas and again on the feast of St John Baptist, because at these two seasons the air is most temperate, but more so at Christmas. And when the year is hotter, and there is less rain, they gather three or four hundred *bahar* of cloves in each of those islands and they grow only in the mountains. And if one of these trees is planted in the low ground near the mountains, it dies. Its leaf, the bark and the green wood are as strong as the clove. And if it be not gathered when it is ripe, it grows so large and hard that only the husk is of any good. Nowhere in the world do good cloves grow except on five mountains of those five islands, but that some are found in the island of Giailolo, and in a small island called Mare, which is between Tadore and Mutir, but they are not good. We saw almost every day a cloud descend and encircle first one of those mountains and then the other, whereby the cloves become more perfect. Each one of those people has trees, and watches over them in his place without cultivating them.

In that island are also some nutmeg trees, the tree of which is like our walnut with the same leaves. And when the nut is gathered, it is as large as a small quince apple, having similar rind and the same colour. Its first rind is as thick as the green rind of our walnut, and under that is a thin loose rind, under which is the mace, very red and wrapped about the rind of the nut, and inside this is the nutmeg.

The houses of those people are built like the others, but not so high from the ground, and they are enclosed and surrounded by bamboos. The women are ugly, and go naked like the others, with these cloths of bark. And those cloths are made after this fashion. They take a piece of bark, which they soak in water until it is soft, then they beat it with wood so that it becomes as long and as wide as they wish. And it is like a cloth of raw silk, with threads in it making it appear as if woven. They eat bread from a tree like the palm, made in this fashion. They take a piece of that soft wood, and draw from it certain long black thorns, then they pound it, and so make bread. And they scarcely use it except when at sea, and they call it *saghu*.* Those men go naked like the others, and are so jealous of their wives that they did not wish us to go ashore with our drawers uncovered. For they said that their women thought that we always had our member in readiness.

Every day there came from Tarenate many boats laden with cloves, but, since we awaited the king, we did not trade in anything

* Sago.

but victuals. Wherefore the people from Tarenate complained much that we refused to trade with them. On Sunday the twenty-fourth of November our king came by night, playing his brass drums, and as he passed through our ships we discharged many of our guns. And when we received him he told us that within four days many cloves would arrive. On Monday the king sent us seven hundred and ninety *cathils* of cloves, without levying the *tara*. The *tara* is to take the spices for less than their weight, because every day they become dryer and waste away. And because these were the first cloves that we had laden in our ships we fired many guns when they came. The clove is called the *ghomode*; in Saranghani, where we took the two pilots, *bonghalanan*; and in Malacca, *chianche*.

On Tuesday the twenty-sixth of November the king told us that it was not the custom for any king to leave his island, but that he had left it for love of the King of Castille. And he begged us to go very soon to Spain, and to return with as many ships as we could in order to avenge the death of his father, who was killed in an island named Buru and then thrown into the sea. And he told us that it was the custom, when the first cloves were loaded on the ships or junks, that the king make a feast and banquet for the men of the ships, and pray to his god to conduct them safe to their port. And he wished to do so because of the King of Bacchian and one of his brothers who were coming to see him, wherefore he had the streets cleaned.

Some of us, supposing that this was some treachery (because, where we took water, three Portuguese servants of Francisco Serrão had been killed by some of those people hidden in the woods, and also because we saw those Indians speaking very low to our captives), were in great doubt and of contrary opinion to those who wished to go to the banquet, saying that we ought not to go ashore and reminding them of another such misfortune. So we wrought on them that it was decided to send to tell the king that he be pleased to come to our ships, since we were about to depart, and to give him the four men whom we had promised him, with other merchandise.

The king came immediately and, entering the ships, he told some of his people that he entered there as safely as into his own houses. Then he said to us that he was greatly amazed that we wished to depart so soon, as the space of time for lading the ships was thirty days, and that he had not departed to do us any ill, but to supply our ships with cloves more quickly. And he besought us that we should not leave at once, seeing that it was not yet the season for navigation among those islands, and also because of the rocks and reefs which were round the island of Bandan, and also because we might easily have encountered some ships of the Portuguese. And, if we were minded to depart at once, he requested us to take all our merchandise, because the kings his neighbours would say that the King of Tadore had received so many gifts from so great a king, and had given him nothing, and they would think that we had departed only for fear of some deception and treachery, whereby he would always be named and reputed a traitor. Then he had his crown* brought and, first kissing it and setting it on his head four or five times, and saying to himself certain words (which actions, when they perform them, are called *zzambachean*†), he said in the presence of all that he swore by Ala, his great god, and by his crown‡ which he had in his hand, that he desired to be forever a very loyal friend of the King of Spain. And he spoke these words almost weeping.

In return for all these good words, we promised him to wait for another fifteen days. And then we gave him the king's signature and the royal banner. But later we heard that some chief men of that island had told him that he should have us killed, and that it would give great pleasure to the Portuguese, and that they would therefore pardon those of Bacchian. To which the king replied that he would not do so for any consideration, knowing the King of Spain and because he had made peace with us and plighted his faith.

★ The Italian Ms. has: 'his Koran'.   † i.e. *subban*, 'giving praise'.
‡ Italian Ms.: 'Koran'.

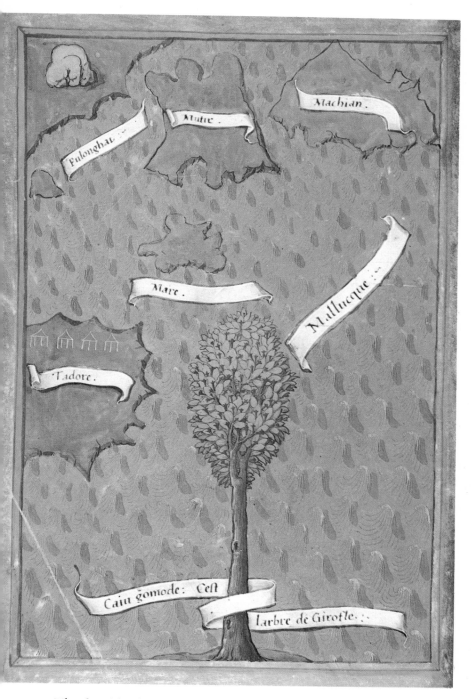

The five islands where grow the cloves, and of their tree.

CHAPTER XL

Of the proclamation that the King of Tadore made. Of the help in cloth that he gave to our men. The Governor of Macchian went to seek cloves. Of the three children of the King of Tarenate. Of the said king, and of the King of Giailolo, and other things.

On Wednesday the twenty-seventh of November the king caused it to be proclaimed that all those who had cloves should carry them to the ships. This was done, so that all that day and the next day we traded and took in cloves with might and main. On Friday, in the evening, the Governor of Macchian arrived with many *prao*, but he would not land, because his father was there, and one of his brothers, who had been banished and driven out of Macchian. On the following day our king with the governor his nephew came on board the ships. And, since we had no more cloth, we sent to request from the king three cubits of his, and he gave them to us, and we presented them with other things to the governor, and at their departure we discharged many guns. After this the king sent us six cubits of red cloth, that we might give them to the governor, and we immediately gave them to him, for which he was very thankful to us and promised to send us many cloves. And this governor was named Humar, and he was twenty-five years of age.

On Sunday the last* day of December this governor departed, and he told us that the King of Tadore had given him silk cloths and other gifts, that he might be more ready and solicitous to send us cloves. And on Wednesday morning (because it was St Barbara's day,† and for the coming of the king) we discharged all the artillery. At night the king came to the shore, and he wished to see how we fired the lances and fire bombs, in which he took great pleasure. On Thursday and Friday we purchased many cloves, both in the city and those brought to the ships. And for four cubits of Frisian cloth they gave us one *bahar* of cloves; for two brass chains worth three sols, a hundred pounds of cloves. At length, having no more goods

---

* Should read 'first'.   † St Barbara is the patron saint of gunners.

for trade, each man gave them one his cap, another his cloak, and some shirts, and others clothing, to have his share of cloves. On Saturday three children of the King of Tarenate with three of his wives, daughters of our king, and Pedro Afonso the Portuguese came on board the ships, where we gave to each of the three a pair of gilt glasses, and to the three ladies scissors and other things. And at their departure we fired several pieces of artillery. Then we sent ashore to the daughter of our king, the wife of the King of Tarenate, many things, because she would not come with the others to the ships. All those people, both men and women, go always unshod.

On Sunday the eighth of December (because it was the day of Our Lady's Conception) we fired many pieces of artillery. And on Monday in the evening our king came to the ships with three women who carried herbs, called *betel*, and no other but the king can take women with him. Then came the King of Giailolo, who wished once more to see us fight together. And a few days later our king told us that he was like a child who was taking milk and knew his sweet mother, who on departing would leave him alone; but that more especially he would remain desolate, because he had already known us and tasted some of the things of Spain. And inasmuch as it must be long before we returned, he besought us very amiably to leave him some pieces of artillery for his defence. Then he advised us that, when we departed, we should not sail except by day, because of many rocks and reefs which are in those islands. But we answered him that to go to Spain we must sail by day and night. To which he said that every day he would pray his god that he lead us to safety. Then he declared to us that the King of Bacchian was to come to marry a brother of his to one of his daughters, begging that we would make some entertainment as a sign of joy, but not to fire the great pieces of artillery for they would have done great damage to our ships, seeing that they were laden.

In those days came Pedro Afonso the Portuguese with his wife and all his goods to be in our ships, where we received him. And two days later there came Checchili de Roix, son of the King of Tarenate, in a well-furnished *prao*, and he asked the Portuguese to go down into it for a little. But he answered that he would not go down into it, because he was coming with us to Spain. Then he of Roix wished to go on board the ships, but we prevented him, because he was a very good friend of the Portuguese captain of Malacca and had come to take this Pedro. Then, having failed, he cried out in a loud voice to those who were with him, and rebuked them for having let him go without his leave.

On Sunday the fifteenth of December in the evening, the King of Bacchian and his brother came in a *prao* with three banks of oars on each side, and they were six score men in all, with many banners of parrot feathers, white, yellow and red, and sounding their brass taborins, that to their sound the rowers should row in time. And there were also two other *prao* of maidens to be presented to his betrothed. When they passed near the ships we saluted them with our artillery, and they in salute to us sailed round the ships and the harbour. And (for that it was the custom of no king to go ashore on another's land) our king came to rejoice with him. And when the King of Bacchian saw him come, he rose from the carpet on which he was seated, and placed himself to one side, and our king refused to sit down upon the carpet, but to the other side, so that neither one nor the other was seated on the carpet. The King of Bacchian gave to our king fifty *patoles*, for that he gave his daughter to his brother for wife. These *patoles* are cloths of gold and silk made in China and highly prized among them. And when one of them dies, his kin and friends (to do him greater honour) clothe themselves in these cloths, for each of which they give three *bahar* of cloves, or more or less according as they are.

The next day our king sent to make a banquet for the King of Bacchian by fifty women, all clad in silk cloths from the waist to the knee; and they went two by two, and a man in the middle. And each bore a large dish full of other small dishes of divers kinds of food. The men carried only the wine in large vessels. And two of the oldest women acted as stewards, setting all in order. In this fashion they walked up to the *prao*, where they presented all their services to the king, who was seated on a carpet under a red and yellow canopy. And at their return those ladies took some of our men, as a diversion; and if the ladies had wished to be freed and released, each of them would have been given her trifle.* After this the king sent us goats, coconuts, wine and other things. And this day we bent new sails on the ships, on which was a cross of St James of Galicia,† with letters which said 'This is the figure of our good fortune'.

CHAPTER XLI

Our men gave some pieces of artillery to the king. The King of Bacchian made peace with them. The gifts which he sent to the King of Spain. Of the night spells of those people. Of their houses newly constructed. Of ginger. Our men in one ship prevented from leaving. Of the king's diligence in remedying this. Of the leave and departure of our men and of the king. And of the goods found in the islands of Molucca. And the description of them.

On Tuesday we gave some pieces of artillery to our king, such as arquebuses which we had taken in those Indies, and some of our hackbuts, with four barrels of powder. And there we took in eighty butts of water for each ship. Five days earlier the king had sent a hundred men to cut wood for us in the island of Mare, since we had to pass that way. And that day the King of Bacchian with many of his people came ashore to make peace with us. Before him marched four men bearing staves or straight swords in their hand. And, our king and all the others being present, he said that he would be forever the servant of the King of Spain, and would keep safe and guard in his name the cloves left by the Portuguese until another of our fleets should return, and that he would never yield them up without our consent.

As a gift to the king he sent a slave and two *bahar* of cloves. He sent ten *bahar*, but our ships were so laden that we could not carry them away. He sent him also two very beautiful dead birds, which

---

* The Italian Ms. has a more intelligible version: 'they took some of our men, and if they wished to be free, it was necessary to give them some trifle'.
† i.e. St James of Compostella.

are as thick as stock-doves with small head and long beak, and legs a palm in length and as thin as a feather. They have no wings, but have instead long feathers of divers colours like large plumes. The tail is as long as that of a stock-dove, and all the other feathers except the wings are of a tawny colour, and they never fly except when there is wind. We were told that those birds came from the earthly paradise, and were called *bolon diuata*, that is to say, birds of God.[*]

All the kings of Molucca wrote to the King of Spain that they desired to be forever his true subjects. The King of Bacchian was sixty years old, and it was his custom, when he went to war or to some other important action, first to have it done two or three times as a trial by one of his servants who was kept expressly for that. One day our king sent to tell our men, who were at the house of the merchandise, that they should not go by night outside the house, because of some of his people who anoint themselves and cast spells and seem to have no heads. And when one of them finds any other man, he touches that man's hand, and as he touches it he anoints it a little, whereupon the man at once becomes ill and dies within three or four days. And when those people find four or five others together, they do them no harm except that they put an enchantment and sorcery on them, so that they make them lose their senses. And [the king] had had many of them hanged.

When the people of that island build a new house, before going to live in it they make a fire all round and many banquets. Then they fasten to the ridge of the house a little of every thing that is found in their island, to the end that those who dwell in it may never want for such things. In all those islands ginger is found, which we ate green like bread. This ginger is not a tree but a small plant which produces and throws out above the ground certain shoots or pipes, a palm in length, like those of reeds, and with the same leaves but narrower and shorter. And these shoots or pipes are worthless, but the root is the ginger, which is not so strong green as when it is dried. And those people dry it in large jars[†] for otherwise it would not keep.

[*] Birds of paradise.

[†] A misreading by the French translator. The Italian Ms. has 'dry it in lime'.

On Wednesday morning, as we desired to leave Molucca, the King of Tadore, the King of Giailolo, the King of Bacchian, and a son of the King of Tarenate had all come to accompany us and conduct us to the island of Mare. Then the ship named Victoria made sail and stood out a little, awaiting the ship Trinidad. But the latter, not being able to weigh anchor, quickly sprang a leak in her bottom, wherefore the Victoria returned to her anchorage, and we began diligently to lighten the Trinidad, to see whether we could repair her. We heard the water entering as if through a pipe, but we could not find the place where it entered.

All that day and the next we did nothing but work at the pump, but all to no purpose. Seeing this, our king came at once to the ship and took pains to discover where the water came in, and he sent five of his men into the water to see whether they could find the hole or aperture, and they were more than half an hour under the water, but never found it. Then the king, seeing that they could not remedy it and that the water always increased, said almost weeping that he would send to the cape of the island to seek three men who could remain under water a long time.

On Friday morning early, our king came with those three men, whom he sent immediately into the water with their long hair loose, so that with their tools they might find the opening and leak. They were a good hour under water, but did not find it. The king, seeing that nothing availed, said weeping, 'Who will go to Spain to give the King my lord news of me?' To which we replied that the Victoria would go in order not to lose the wind which was beginning to rise, and that the other ship, until she was refitted, would await the west wind, and would then go to Darien (which is on the other side of the sea) in the land of Yacutan.* Then the king said that he

---

* Leaving a small party at Tidore, the *Trinidad* and her crew, commanded by Gonzalo Gómez de Espinosa, sailed on 6 April 1522 and, reaching the Marianas, continued on a northeast course to about 43°N, where, having lost three-fifths of his men from sickness, Espinosa turned back in August. Reaching the Moluccas early in November, he surrendered to António de Brito who had on 13 May arrived at Ternate with seven ships and established himself

had two hundred and twenty-five workmen and shipwrights, who would refit her entirely, and that, for those of our men who would remain there, he would tend and treat them like his children, and that they would suffer no other fatigue, but to give orders to the workmen and show them what they had to do. The king spoke these words with so much passion and sorrow that he caused us all to weep. Then we feared lest the ship Victoria open and split by being overladen, wherefore we lightened her of sixty quintals of cloves, which we caused to be carried into the house where the rest were. Some men of our ship wished to remain there for fear that she could not endure and go all the way to Spain; but it was rather for fear of dying of hunger.

On Saturday the twenty-first of December, St Thomas's day, our king came to the ships, and gave us the two pilots whom we had paid to conduct us out of these islands, and they told us that this hour was a good time to sail. But because our men who remained wished to write letters to Spain, we could not sail until after noon. The time being come, the ships took leave one of another by firing of guns, and it seemed that they were lamenting their last parting. And our men who were to remain accompanied us a little way in the boats. Then with many tears and embraces we departed. The king's governor came with us as far as the island of Mare,★ where we had no sooner arrived than we bought four *prao* loaded with wood, which in less than an hour we loaded into the ships. Then we forthwith laid course to the southwest. And João Carvalho remained there with fifty of our men.† And we were no more than forty-seven, and thirteen Indians. That island of Tadore has a bishop, and at this

★ Mare, off the south coast of Tidore.
† João Carvalho had already been succeeded in command of the fleet in September 1521 by Espinosa, who also remained behind at Tidore with fifty-three men. Carvalho died there on 14 February 1522, before the *Trinidad* sailed.

there. Of the twenty-three prisoners taken by the Portuguese and eventually sent back to Europe, only Espinosa and three others returned to Spain in 1525.

time he was aged forty-five years and had forty wives and many children.

In all those islands of Molucca are found ginger, sago which is their bread made from wood, rice, goats, geese, poultry, coconuts, figs, almonds larger than ours, sweet pomegranates, oranges, lemons, honey from bees, as small as ants, who make their honey in trees, sugarcanes, coconut oil and beneseed oil, melons, cucumbers, sugar, a refreshing fruit as large as a gourd, called *comulicai*,★ and another fruit which is rather like a peach, named *guaue*, and other things to eat. There are also to be found there parrots of divers sorts: some white, called *catara*, and others all red called *nori*. One of the red ones is valued at a *bahar* of cloves, and they speak more distinctly and better than the others. The Moors have lived in Molucca for about fifty years, and before that heathen lived there, who had not put a value and price on the cloves. There are still some there, but they abide in the mountains where the cloves grow.

The island of Tadore is in the latitude of twenty-seven minutes toward the Antarctic Pole, and in the longitude of one hundred and sixty-one degrees from the line of partition, and it is nine and a half degrees to the south of the first island of the archipelago, called Zzamal, lying northeast, and southwest.

Tarenate is two-thirds of a degree toward the Antarctic Pole.

Mutir is exactly under the Equinoctial line.

Macchian is one quarter of a degree toward the Antarctic Pole.

And Bacchian is one degree toward the Antarctic Pole.† Tarenate, Tadore, Mutir and Macchian form four high peaked mountains, where the cloves grow. And from those four islands one cannot see Bacchian, although it is larger than each of those four islands. And its mountain of cloves is not as pointed as the others, but it is larger.

★ Apparently mango.
† Modern names and determinations of latitude: Ternate 0°40′S, Tidore 0°50′N, Moti 0°26′N, Makian 0°20′N, Batjan 0°39′–1°S.

Here follow some words of those heathen peoples of Molucca★

Their god *Alla*

Christian *Naceran*

Turk *Rumno*

Moor *Musulman, Isilam*

Heathen *Caphre*

Their mosques *Mischit*

Their priests *Maulana catip mudin*

Wise men *Horan pandita*

Their pious men *Mossai*

Their ceremonies *Zambahehan de ala meschit*

The father *Bapa*

The mother *Mama ambui*

The son *Anach*

The brother *Saudala*

The brother of so-and-so *Capatin muiadi*

The cousin *Saudala sopopu*

Grandfather *Niny*

Father-in-law *Minthua*

Son-in-law *Mi nanthu*

Man *Horan*

Woman *Poran poan*

The hair *Lambut*

The head *Capala*

The forehead *Dai*

The eye *Matta*

The eyebrows *Quilai*

The eyelids *Cenin*

The nose *Idon*

The mouth *Mulut*

The lips *Bebere*

The teeth *Gigi*

The cheeks *Issi*

The tongue *Lada*

The palate *Langhi*

The chin *Aghai*

The beard *Janghut*

The moustaches *Missai*

The jaw *Pipi*

The ear *Talingha*

The throat *Laher*

The neck *Tun dun*

The shoulders *Balachan*

The breast *Dada*

The heart *Atti*

The teat *Sussu*

The stomach *Parut*

The body *Tun dunbutu*

The penis *Botto*

The vagina *Bucchii*

To cohabit with women *Amput*

The buttocks *Buri*

The thighs *Taha*

The leg *Mina*

The shin of the leg *Tula*

Its calf *Tilor chaci*

★ Under this heading, the Beinecke Ms. repeats the vocabulary of Cebu (pp. 97–99). For the sake of completeness, the Malay vocabulary collected in the Moluccas is printed below from the Italian Ms., with translation of the English equivalents. Pigafetta's vocabulary is accurate and is one of the oldest extant (written) specimens of the Malay language.

The ankle *Buculati*
The heel *Tumi*
The foot *Batis*
The sole of the foot *Empachaqui*
The fingernail *Cuchu*
The arm *Langhan*
The elbow *Sichu*
The hand *Tanghan*
The large finger [thumb]
    Idun tanghan
The second finger *Tungu*
The third *Geri*
The fourth *Mani*
The fifth *Calinchin*
Rice *Bugax*
Coconut, in Molucca and
    Burne *Biazzao*
[Coconut] in Lozon *Nior*
[Coconut] in Java Major
    Calambil
Fig [i.e. banana] *Pizan*
Sugercane *Tubu*
Batate *Gumbili*
The roots like turnips *Ubi*
Nangca *Mandicai sicui*
Melon *Antimon*
Cucumbers *Labu*
Cow *Lambu*
Hog *Babi*
Buffalo *Carban*
Sheep *Biri*
She goat *Cambin*
Cock *Sambunghan*
Hen *Aimbatina*
Capon *Gubili*

Egg *Talor*
Gander *Itich*
Goose *Ansa*
Bird *Bolon*
Elephant *Gagia*
Horse *Cuda*
Lion *Huriman*
Deer *Roza*
Reeds *Cuiu*
Bees *Haermadu*
Honey *Gulla*
Wax *Lelin*
Candle *Dian*
Its wick *Sumbudian*
Fire *Appi*
Smoke *Asap*
Ashes *Abu*
Cooked *Azap*
Much cooked *Lambech*
Water *Tubi*
Gold *Amax*
Silver *Pirac*
Precious stone *Premata*
Pearl *Mutiara*
Quicksilver *Raza*
Metal [copper] *Tumbaga*
Iron *Baci*
Lead *Tima*
Their gongs *Agun*
Cinnabar *Galuga sadalinghan*
Silver [cloth?] *Soliman danas*
Silk cloth *Cain sutra*
Red cloth *Cain mira*
Black cloth *Cain ytam*
White cloth *Cain pute*

Green cloth *Cain igao*
Yellow cloth *Cain cunin*
Cap *Cophia*
Knife *Pixao*
Scissors *Guntin*
Mirror *Chiela min*
Comb *Sissir*
Glass bead *Manich*
Bell *Giringirin*
Ring *Sinsin*
Cloves *Ghianche*
Cinnamon *Caiumanis*
Pepper *Lada*
Long pepper *Sabi*
Nutmeg *Buapala gosoga*
Copper wire *Canot*
Dish *Pinghan*
Earthen pot *Prin*
Porringer *Manchu*
Wooden dish *Dulan*
Shell *Calunpan*
Their measures *Socat*
Land *Buchit*
Mainland *Buchit tana*
Mountain *Gonun*
Rock *Batu*
Island *Polan*
A cape of land *Taniun buchit*
River *Songhai*
What is this man's name?
   Apenamaito?
Coconut oil *Mignach*
Beneseed oil *Lana lingha*
Salt *Garan sira*
Musk and its animal *Castori*

The wood eaten by 'castori'
   Comaru
Leech *Linta*
Civet *Jabat*
The cat which makes the civet
   Mozan
Rhubarb *Calama*
Demon *Saytan*
The world *Bumi*
Wheat *Gandun*
To sleep *Tidor*
Mats *Tical*
Cushion *Bantal*
Pain *Sachet*
Health *Bay*
Brush *Cupia*
Fan *Chipas*
Their cloths *Chebun*
Shirts *Bain*
Their houses *Pati alam*
Year *Tanu*
Month *Bullan*
Day *Alli*
Night *Mallan*
Afternoon *Malamari*
Noon *Tam hahari*
Morning *Patan patan*
Sun *Mata hari*
Moon *Bulan*
Half moon *Tanam patbulan*
Stars *Bintan*
Sky *Languin*
Thunder *Gunthur*
Merchant *Sandgar*
City *Naghiri*

Castle *Cuta*
House *Rinna*
To sit *Duodo*
Sit down, sir *Duodo orancaia*
Sit down, good fellow *Duodo*
 horandai et anan
Lord *Tuan*
Boy *Cana Cana*
One of their foster children
 Lascar
Slave *Alipin*
Yes *Ca*
No *Tida*
To understand *Thao*
Not to understand *Tida taho*
Do not look at me *Tida liat*
Look at me *Liat*
To be one and the same thing
 Casi casi Siama siama
To kill *Mati*
To eat *Macan*
Spoon *Sandoch*
Harlot *Sondal*
Large *Bassal*
Long *Pangian*
Small *Chechil*
Short *Pandach*
To have *Ada*
Not to have *Tidi hada*
Listen, sir *Tuan diam*
Whither goes the junk?
 Dimana ajun?
Sewing needle *Jalun*
To sew *Banan*
Sewing thread *Pintal banan*

Woman's headdress *Dastar capala*
King *Raia*
Queen *Putli*
Wood *Caiu*
To work *Caraiar*
To take recreation *Buandala*
The vein of the where one is
 bled *Urat paratanghan*
The blood that comes from the
 arm *Dara carnal*
Good blood *Dara*
When they sneeze, they say
 Ebarasai
Fish *Ycam*
Polypus *Calabutan*
Meat *Dagin*
Sea snail *Cepot*
Little *Serich*
Half *Satanha sapanghal*
Cold *Dinghin*
Hot *Panas*
For *Jan*
Truth *Benar*
Lie *Dusta*
To steal *Manchiuri*
Scab *Codis*
Take *Na*
Give me *Ambil*
Fat *Gannich*
Thin *Golos*
Hair *Tundun capala*
How many? *Barapa?*
Once *Satu chali*
One cubit *Dapa*
To speak *Catha*

Here *Siui*

There *Sana datan*

Good day *Salamalichum*

And the answer *Alichum salam*

Sirs, good fortune attend you
  Mali horancaia mancan

I have eaten already *Suda macan*

Fellow, take yourself off *Pandan chita horan*

To desire *Banunchan*

Good evening *Sabalchaer*

And the answer *Chaer sandat*

To give *Minta*

To give to some one *Bri pocol*

Iron fetters *Balanghu*

O what a smell! *Bosso chini*

Young man *Horan muda*

Old man *Tua*

Scribe *Xiritoles*

Writing paper *Cartas*

To write *Mangurat*

Pen *Calam*

Ink *Dauat*

Writing desk *Padantan*

Letter *Surat*

I do not have it *Guala*

Come here *Camari*

What do you want? *Appa man?*

Who sent you? *Appa ito?*

Seaport *Labuan*

Galley *Gurap*

Ship *Capal*

Bow [of a boat] *Asson*

Stern [of a boat] *Biritan*

To sail *Belaiar*

Ship's mast *Tian*

Yard [of a ship] *Laiar*

Rigging *Tamira*

Sail *Leier*

Maintop *Sinbulaia*

Anchor rope *Danda*

Anchor *San*

Boat *Sanpan*

Oar *Daiun*

Mortar [cannon] *Badil*

Wind *Anghin*

Sea *Laut*

Fellow, come here *Horan itu datan*

Their daggers *Calix golog*

Their dagger hilt *Daga nan*

Sword *Padan gole*

Blowpipe *Sumpitan*

Their arrows *Damach*

The poisonous herb *Ypu*

Quiver *Bolo*

Bow [weapon] *Bolsor*

Its arrows *Anat paan*

Cats *Cochin puchia*

Rat *Ticus*

Lizard *Buaia*

Shipworms *Capan lotos*

Fishhook *Matacanir*

Fishbait *Unpan*

Fishline *Tunda*

To wash *Mandi*

Not to be afraid *Tangan tacut*

Fatigue *Lala*

A pleasant cup *Sadap manis*

Friend *Sandara*

Enemy *Sanbat*

I am certain *Zonhu*

To barter *Biniaga*

I have not *Anis*

To be a friend *Pugna*

Two things *Malupho*

If *Oue*

Crowd (?) *Zoroan pagnoro*

To give pleasure *Mamain*

To be stiff with cold *Amala*

Madam *Gila*

Interpreter *Giorobaza*

How many languages do you know? *Barapa bahasa tan?*

Many *Bagna*

To speak of Malacca *Chiaramalain*

Where is so-and-so? *Dimana horan?*

Flag *Tonghol*

Now *Sacaran*

Tomorrow *Hezoch*

The next day *Luza*

Yesterday *Calamari*

Palm-mallet *Colbasi*

Nail *Pacu*

Mortar *Lozon*

Pestle for crushing [rice?] *Atan*

To dance *Manari*

To pay *Baiar*

To call *Panghil*

Unmarried *Ugan*

Married *Suda babini*

All one *Sannia*

Rain *Ugian*

Drunken *Moboch*

Skin *Culit*

Anger *Ullat*

To fight *Guzar*

Sweet *Mams*

Bitter *Azon*

How are you? *Appa giadi?*

Well *Bay*

Ill *Sachet*

Bring me that *Biriacan*

This man is a coward *Giadi hiat horan itu*

Enough *Suda*

THE WINDS

North *Iraga*

South *Salatan*

East *Timor*

West *Baratapat*

Northeast *Utara*

Southwest *Berdaia*

Northwest *Bardaut*

Southeast *Tunghara*

NUMBERS

One *Satus*

Two *Dua*

Three *Tiga*

Four *Ampat*

Five *Lima*

Six *Anam*

Seven *Tugu*

Eight *Duolappan*

Nine *Sambilan*

Ten *Sapolo*

Twenty *Duapolo*

Thirty *Tigapolo*

Forty *Ampatpolo*

Fifty *Limapolo*

Sixty *Anampolo*

Seventy *Tuguppolo*

Eighty *Dualapanpolo*

Ninety *Sambilampolo*

One hundred *Saratus*

Two hundred *Duaratus*

Three hundred *Tigaratus*

Four hundred *Anamparatus*

Five hundred *Limaratus*

Six hundred *Anambratus*

Seven hundred *Tugurattus*

Eight hundred *Dualapanratus*

Nine hundred *Sambilanratus*

One thousand *Salibu*

Two thousand *Dualibu*

Three thousand *Tigalibu*

Four thousand *Ampatlibu*

Five thousand *Limalibu*

Six thousand *Anamlibu*

Seven thousand *Tugulibu*

Eight thousand *Dualapanlibu*

Nine thousand *Sambilanlibu*

Ten thousand *Salacza*

Twenty thousand *Dualacza*

Thirty thousand *Tigalacza*

Forty thousand *Ampatlacza*

Fifty thousand *Limalacza*

Sixty thousand *Anamlacza*

Seventy thousand *Tugulacza*

Eighty thousand *Dualapanlacza*

Ninety thousand *Sambilanlacza*

One hundred thousand *Sacati*

Two hundred thousand *Duacati*

Three hundred thousand *Tigacati*

Four hundred thousand *Ampatcati*

Five hundred thousand *Limacati*

Six hundred thousand *Anamcati*

Seven hundred thousand *Tugucati*

Eight hundred thousand *Dualapancati*

Nine hundred thousand *Sambilancati*

One million *Sainta*

CHAPTER XLII

Of the island of Caphi where are the Pygmies. Of the island of Sullac and its inhabitants. Of the other like islands. Of the island of Buru and the things that grow there. And of the island of Ambon, etc.

Going on our way we passed between those islands of Caioan, Laigoma, Gioggi, and Caphi.* In that island of Caphi grow men as small as dwarfs, who are very merry. And they are called Pygmies, and are subjected by force to our King of Tadore.

Passing Labuan, Tolimau, Titameti, Bacchian already mentioned, Latalata, Taboli, Maga and Batutiga,† by the west of Batutiga we sailed between west and southwest and discovered some small islands to the south. And because the pilots of Molucca warned us that there were many rocks and reefs in those islands, we went to the southeast, and anchored at an island which is in the latitude of two degrees and fifty minutes toward the Antarctic Pole and five leagues from Molucca, and is named Sullach.‡ The men of this island are heathen, and they have no king. They eat human flesh and go naked, both men and women, but they wear only a piece of bark two fingers wide before their shameful parts. There are many islands round about, whose inhabitants eat human flesh. And the names of some of them are Silan, Nosselao, Biga, Atulabau, Leitimor, Tenctun, Gondia, Pailarurun, Manadan, and Benaia.§ Then we coasted two islands called Lumatola‖ and Tentenun.

About ten leagues from Sullach on the same course we discovered a fairly large island,¶ in which there are rice, swine, goats,

* Islands of the archipelago between Makian and Batjan. Modern names: Kajoa, Laigoma, Gumorga (?), Gafi.

† Islands to the west and south of Batjan, tentatively identified as Labuha (the southern part of Batjan), Tawali bezar, Tawali ketyl, Batjan, Latalata, Tappi (?), Lumang (?), Obi.

‡ Sula Besi, in the Sula group, southeast of Obi, and much more than 'five leagues from Molucca'.

§ These island names are very confused; some appear to belong to the Sula group, others to the waters round Ambon.

‖ Lifamatola.   ¶ Buru.

poultry, coconuts, sugarcanes, sago, a food made from figs and almonds and honey wrapped in leaves, dried in the smoke and made into fairly long pieces, and it is called *canali*. The people of this island go naked like those of Sullach. They are heathens and have no king. This island is in the latitude of three and a half degrees toward the Antarctic Pole, and sixty-five leagues distant from Molucca, and it is named Buru. And ten leagues to the east of this island is another larger one near to Giailolo, which is inhabited by Moors and by heathen. The Moors are near the sea, and the heathen inland. And the latter eat human flesh. In this island grow the aforesaid things, and it is called Ambon. And between Buru and Ambon are three islands surrounded by rocks and reefs, called Vudia, Cailarury and Benaia. And about four leagues midway to Buru is a small island named Ambalao.*

CHAPTER XLIII

Of the island of Bandan, containing twelve islands, where grow mace and nutmeg. Of the names of the said islands, and of the things found there.

About thirty-five leagues from that island of Buru, to the south by west is Bandan.† Bandan consists of twelve islands, in six of which grow mace and nutmeg. And their names are Zzorobua, which is larger than all the others, Chelicel, Samanapi, Pulae, Pulurun and Rossonghin. The other six are these: Unuueru, Pulaubaracan, Lailaca, Manucan, Man and Meut. In these six are no mace, but only sago, rice, coconuts, figs and other fruit, and they lie close to one another. The people of these islands are Moors, and have no king. Bandan is in the latitude of six degrees toward the Antarctic Pole, and in the longitude of one hundred and sixty-three and a half degrees from the partition line. And because it was somewhat distant and out of our way, we did not go there.

* Ambelou.
† The Banda group; in fact ESE of Buru, and in 4½°S. A few of the names which follow are easily identifiable: *Pulae*, Ai; *Pulurun*, Run; *Rossonghin*, Rosengain.

CHAPTER XLIV

Storms and impediments which our men had among some islands. Of the island of Mallua to which they came. The manner of life and habits of the people of that island, their attire, their bows. And of the long pepper that grows there.

D eparting from that island of Buru, [and sailing] on a course south-west by west over about eight degrees of longitude, we came to three islands close to one another, called Zzolot, Nocemanor, and Galiau.★ And as we sailed through the midst of them, a great storm assailed and struck us, wherefore we made a pilgrimage to Our Lady of Guidance. And with the gale on our poop we anchored at a high island, but before reaching it we were in great travail for the very strong winds and currents of water which came down from their mountains.

The men of this island are savage and bestial. They eat human flesh, and have no king. And they go naked, with that bark like the others; but when they go to war, they wear certain pieces of oxhide before, behind and at the sides, decorated with small shells and swine's teeth, and with tails of goatskins fastened before and behind. They wear their hair high, with some pins of bamboo which pass through it from side to side, and so keep it high. They wear their beards wrapped in leaves and thrust into small bamboos, which is a thing ridiculous to see. And they are the ugliest people who are in those Indies. Their bows and arrows are of bamboo, and they have certain sacks of leaves of trees, in which they carry their food and drink. And when their women saw us, they came to meet us with their bows. But after we had given them some presents, we were immediately their friends. And we remained there fifteen days to refit our ships.

★ Solor, Nobokamor Rusa, and Lomblen. The ship had cross the Banda Sea (in fact traversing no more than four degrees of latitude, half of Pigafetta's reckoning) and come to the island chain of the Sundas extending from Sumatra to Timor. The passage taken by the *Victoria* was Boleng Strait or Flores Strait, to the east or west of Solor; and thence they sailed east to Alor, reaching it on 10 January 1522.

In this island are poultry, goats, coconuts, and wax. There is found also long pepper, and tree of which is like ivy, which twists itself and clings like it to trees. But the leaves are like those of the mulberry, and they call it *luli*. Round pepper grows like it, but in ears like Indian corn, from which it is shelled off; and they call it *lada*. And in those countries the fields are all full of this pepper. There we took a man to guide us to some island where there would be provisions. The said island is in the latitude of eight and a half degrees toward the Antarctic Pole, and in the longitude of one hundred and sixty-nine and two thirds degrees from the line of partition; and it is named Mallua.*

CHAPTER XLV

Of the men and women of the island of Aruchete. Of the lord of the town of Amabau, and of its inhabitants. Of white sandalwood. And of the four islands of Oibich, Suai, Lichsana and Cabinazza.

Our old pilot of Molucca told us that nearby was an island named Aruchete, where the men and women are no taller than a cubit and have ears so large that of one they make their bed, and with the other they cover themselves. They are shaven and quite naked, and run swiftly, and have shrill and thin voices. They live in caves underground. They eat fish and a thing which grows between the barks of trees, which is white and round like a sugarplum and which they call *ambulon*. We could not go thither by reason of the strong currents and the many reefs which are there.

On Saturday the twenty-fifth of January, one thousand five hundred and twenty-two, we departed from the island of Mallua. And on the Sunday following we came to a large island† five leagues distant from the other, between south and southwest. And I went ashore alone to speak to the chief man of a town named Amabau,‡ that he might give us provisions. He answered that he would give

* Alor; here they remained for fifteen days.
† Timor.   ‡ Ambeno.

us oxen, pigs and goats; but we could not agree together, because he desired, for an ox, too many things of which we had little. Wherefore, since hunger constrained us, we retained in our ships one of their principal men with a son of his, who was from another town called Balibo.* And, fearing lest we kill them, they gave us six oxen, five goats and two pigs, and to complete the number of ten pigs and ten goats they gave us an ox, for we had set them to this ransom. Then we sent them ashore very well pleased, for we gave them linen, cloths of silk and of cotton, knives, scissors, mirrors and other things.

This lord of Amabau, to whom I spoke, had only women to serve him. They go all naked like the others, and wear in their ears little gold rings hanging from silk threads, and on their arms, up to the elbow, they have many bracelets of gold and of cotton.† And the men go like the women, but that they have and wear on their neck certain gold rings as large and round as a trencher, and set in their hair bamboo combs garnished with gold. And some of them wear other gold ornaments. In this island, and nowhere else, is found white sandalwood,‡ besides ginger, oxen, swine, goats, poultry, rice, figs, sugarcanes, oranges, lemons, wax, almonds and other things, and parrots of divers sorts and colours. On the other side of this island are four brothers, its kings. And where we were there are only towns, and some chiefs and lords of them. The names of the habitations of the four kings are: Oibich, Lichsana, Suai, and Cabanazza.§ Oibich is the largest town. In Cabanazza (as we were told) a quantity of gold is found in a mountain, and they purchase all their things with certain small gold pieces which they have. All the sandalwood and the wax which is traded by the people of Java and Malacca comes from this place, where we found a junk of Lozzon‖ which had come to trade for sandalwood.

* Silabão.
† A misreading for 'brass'.
‡ Sandalwood is found in other islands, though principally in Timor.
§ Places on the south side of Timor.
‖ Luzon, in the Philippines.

CHAPTER XLVI

The manner of cutting sandalwood, and of the devil who appeared there. This sandalwood grows in the island of Timor. Of the said island. And of St Job's disease that prevails there.

 he peoples of the aforesaid places are heathen, and when they go to cut the sandalwood (as they told us) the devil appears in divers forms, who tells them, if they have need of anything, to demand it of him. Because of this apparition they are sick for some days. The sandalwood is cut at a certain phase of the moon, for otherwise it would not be good. And the goods which are commonly taken in trade for the sandalwood are red cloth, linen, steel, iron and nails.

All this island is inhabited, and it is very long from east to west but not very wide from south to north. It is in the latitude of ten degrees toward the Antarctic Pole, and in the longitude of one hundred and sixty-four and a half degrees from the line of partition, and it is named Timor. In all the islands which we found in that archipelago the disease of St Job★ prevails, and more there than in any other place. They call it *for franchi*, that is to say, the Portuguese disease.

CHAPTER XLVII

Of the islands as far as Java. Of the towns of Java. Of the burial of the great lords of Java. Of the women of the island of Ocoloro. Of the birds called Garuda. Of Malacca and of the cities about it. Of rhubarb, where it grows. Of the King of China the Great. Of that king's marriage. Of his palace and halls. And of the people of China. And of musk.

 e were told that, at a distance of a day's sail thence between west and northwest, we should find an island in which grows a quantity of cinnamon, and it is named Ende,† and that its people are

★ St Job's disease was a name applied in Europe to syphilis, generally supposed to have been introduced from Haiti by Columbus and his men. There is a possible confusion with yaws, also endemic in the Pacific islands before European discovery. † Flores.

heathen and have no king, and that in the same course are many
islands, one after the other, as far as Java the Great and the Cape of
Malacca. These are their names: Ende, Tanabuntin, Crevo, Chile,
Bimacore, Aranaran, Moin, Zzunbava, Lomboch, Chorun and Java
the Great.*

Those peoples call it not Java, but Jaoa. And the largest towns
which are in Java are these: Maggepaher, the king of which, while
he lived, was the greatest of all these islands, and was named Raia
Patiuaus† Sunda, and much pepper grows there. The others are:
Daha, Dama, Gaggiamada, Minutaranghan, Cipara, Sidaiu, Tuban,
Cressi, Cirubaia, and Balli.‡ And we were also told that Java the
Little was the island of Madura, and a half league from Java the
Great.

When one of the principal men of Java the Great dies, his body is
burned, and his principal wife, adorned with chaplets of flowers, has
herself borne on a chair by three or four men through the whole
town, and laughing and comforting her kinsfolk who weep and sigh,
she says: Weep not, for I go this evening to sup with my dear
husband. Then, being at the place where the said body is being
burned, she turns to her relatives and, comforting them once more,
she throws herself into the fire where the body of her husband is
burning. And, if she did not do so, she would never be thought a
woman of honour nor a true wife of her dead husband.§ Our oldest

* The first seven of these names probably represent islands of the Sunda chain
westward from Flores (*Ende*) to Sumbawa (*Zzunbava*), Lombok, Bali (*Chorun*),
and Java. Marco Polo, the first European to pick up the name Java, dis-
tinguished Java the Great from Java the Lesser, i.e. Sumatra.
† The Italian Ms., more correctly, indicates Sunda as the second 'town' listed,
and not part of the king's name.
‡ The cities or districts of Java and the adjacent islands named in this para-
graph, are identified as Majapahit (the capital), Sunda (probably western
Java, inhabited by Sundanese), Daha (in eastern Java), Demak, [two un-
identified places], Japara, Tuban, Geresik, Surabaya, Bali.
§ This concremation, akin to Buddhist rites in Siam and to Hindu suttee, was
peculiar to the people of Bali and not practised in Java.
    Here the other Mss. have a paragraph which is omitted from the Beinecke
Ms.: 'When the young men of Java are in love with any gentlewoman, they

pilot told us that in an island called Ocoloro,* below Java the Great, there are only women, who become pregnant with wind. And when they give birth, if the child is male they kill it, and if it is a girl they rear it. And if any men come into that island, they kill them if they can.

The pilots told us also that below Java the Great to the north, in the gulf of China (which the ancients call Sino Magno†), is a very tall tree in which dwell birds, called *garuda*, so large that they carry off an ox or an elephant from the place where the tree is.‡ This place is called *Puzzathaer*, the tree *caiu paugganghi*, and its fruit *bua paugganghi*, which is larger than a cucumber. The Moors from Burne whom we had in our ships told us that they had seen them, because two of them had been sent to their king from the kingdom of Siam. No junk or other boat can come within three or four leagues of the place of the tree (for the great storms of water around it). And the first time that anything was known of this tree, it was by a junk which was driven by the force of the winds ashore at that place, where it was all broken and perished and all the men were drowned except one little boy. Having set himself on a plank of wood, he was by a miracle sent near that tree, and climbing up into it he seated himself, without noticing, beneath the wing of one of those birds. And the next day, the bird having flown to the ground and taken an ox, the boy escaped from beneath its wing as best he could. And so all this became known. And then the people of the neighbourhood knew that the fruit which they found by the sea came from that tree.

* Perhaps Enggano, off the southwest coast of Sumatra.
† Ptolemy's Sinus Magnus.
‡ An Arab fable, found in the Arabian Nights.

---

bind certain little bells with thread under their foreskin. They go beneath their loved ones' window and, making pretence to urinate and shaking the member, they ring the little bells until their loved ones hear the sound. Then they come down immediately, and they take their pleasure, always with those little bells, for their women take great delight in hearing those bells ring within. Those bells are all covered, and the more they are covered the louder they ring.'

The Cape of Malacca is in one and a half degrees toward the Antarctic Pole.⋆ And to the east of this cape, along the coast, there are many towns and cities, the names of some of which are: Cinghapola, which is at the cape, Pahan, Calantan, Patani, Braadlun, Benan, Lagon, Chereggiegharan, Tumbon, Pihan, Cui, Brabri, Bangha, Iudia (and this is the city where dwells the king of Siam, named Siri), then Zzacabedera, Jundibun, Langonpipha, and Lauu.† These cities are built like ours and are subject to the King of Siam. On the riverbanks in this kingdom of Siam (as we were told) live large birds which do not eat of any dead animal carried there unless there come first another bird which eats the heart, and afterward they eat the rest.

After Siam you find Camogia,‡ the king of which is called Saret Zzacabedera, and Chiempa,§ which has a king called Raia Brahaun Maitri. In that place grows rhubarb, which is found in this manner. Twenty or twenty-five men gather and go together into the woods, and coming there they climb into trees as well to smell the scent of the rhubarb as for fear of lions, elephants and other wild beasts; and from the place where the rhubarb is the wind brings its odour. Then, day being come, they go into that part whence by scent they knew the wind to have blown, and there they search until they find it.

The rhubarb is a large and rotten tree, and if it were not rotten it would not give off the odour; and the best of that tree is the root, but the wood is rhubarb to which they give the name *calama*. Then you find Cocchi,‖ the king of which is called Raia Seribunnipala.

⋆ A mistake for 'Arctic Pole', if the southern extremity of the Malay Peninsula is intended.
† These places or countries, Pigafetta's names for most of which are easily recognizable in the modern forms, lie along the east side of the Malay Peninsula or in the Gulf of Siam. *Iudia* is Yuthia or Ayutthaya, the ancient capital of Siam.
‡ Cambodia.
§ Champa, a Malay kingdom between Cambodia and Cochinchina, on the east side of the Gulf of Siam.
‖ Cochinchina.

Near this you find China the Great, the king of which is the greatest in all the world and is named Santhoa Raia.* This king has seventy crowned kings under him. His port is called Guantua.† And of the other cities, which are very numerous, there are two principal ones, named Namchin and Commilaha,‡ in which this king dwells. He has four of his principal men near his palace, one toward the east, another to the west, another to the south, and another toward the north. Each of them gives audience only to those who come from his own quarter.

All the kings and lords of Greater India and of Upper India obey this king, and for a sign that they are his true vassals each of them has in the middle of his square a beast graved in marble, handsomer and bolder than a lion, and it is called *cingha*.§ And this *cingha* is the seal of the King of China. And all those who go to China must have this engraved beast impressed on wax [or?] on an elephant's tooth, otherwise they could not enter his port. When any lord disobeys this king, they have him flayed and his skin dried in the sun with salt, then they fill it with straw or some other thing and set it up with its head downward and hands clasped on the head. Then they display it at a prominent place in the public square, that it may be seen as an example.

This king does not permit himself to be seen by anyone. And when he wishes to see his people, he rides through the palace on a peacock made by great mastery and craft (a thing very rich), and he is accompanied by six of his principal women attired like him. So he goes until he enters a serpent called *nagha*, also made by artifice, and as rich a thing as one could see, which is in the largest court of his palace. And the king enters it, and his women, that he be not recognized among them. And so he sees all his people through a great glass which is in the chest of the serpent, where he and his women can be seen, but he cannot be recognized.

* The Emperor Chitsong, of the Ming dynasty, reigned 1519–64. Pigafetta's account of China which follows leans heavily on Marco Polo.
† Canton.   ‡ Nanking and Cambaluc (Peking).
§ The dragon, emblem of China.

This king marries his sisters, that the royal blood be not mingled with any other. And round his palace are seven enclosures or circles of walls, each of which has ten thousand men who stand guard on the palace until a bell is rung, when at its sound ten thousand other men come for each circle. And so his guards are changed each day and night. Each circle or enclosure of the wall has a gate. At the first stands a porter holding in his hand a large thick stick, called *satu horan*. In the second gate is a dog, called *satu hain*. In the third, a man with an iron mace, called *satu bagan*. And in the fourth, a man with a bow in his hand, called *satu horan*. In the fifth, a man with a lance, called *satu horan*. In the sixth, a lion, called *satu huriman*. And in the seventh, two white elephants, called *gaggia pute*.

In this palace are seventy-nine halls, where dwell only the women who serve the king, and there are always burning torches there. And in the topmost part are four halls, where the principal men sometimes go to visit the king and to speak with him. One of these halls is adorned with metal [copper] both below and above, another all with silver, another all with gold, and another with pearls and precious stones. When this king's vassals bring him gold or other rich things as tribute, he has them placed in these halls, those who bring them saying, 'Let this be to the honour of our Santhor Raia.' All these things and many others were told to us by a Moor, who said that he had seen them.

The people of China are white and clothed, and they eat from tables as we do, and they have crosses but know not the reason why they keep them. And musk grows there, the animal of which is like a cat, and it eats nothing but a sweet and tender wood, as thin as fingers, called *commaru*. And when they wish to make musk, they attach a leech to the cat, and they leave it attached to it until the leech be full of blood, when they squeeze it into a dish and set the blood in the sun for four or five days. Afterward they steep it in the urine of the cat, and set it as many days again in the sun, and so it becomes perfect musk. Every man who keeps these animals is constrained to give a certain tribute to the king. And those small round pieces which seem to be musk are made from goatflesh crushed with a little musk. But the true musk is of the aforesaid blood, and if it becomes little round grains it is spoilt. And the musk and the cat are called *castori*, and the leech *linta*.

CHAPTER XLVIII

Of the Lechii who are on the mainland, and of their king. Of the island of Hau and others. Of ten kinds of men who are in India the Great. Our men navigated the Cape of Good Hope. Of their suffering and mortality in the ships. Trick played by our men on the Portuguese to obtain victuals. Thirteen of our men were detained by the Portuguese. Our men arrived at Seville, where they made their vows. And the author parted from them to go his way.

Then following the coast of China we discovered many peoples, who are these. The Chienchii* dwell in the islands where grow pearls and cinnamon. The Lechii† are on the mainland, and above its port extends a mountain, wherefore all the junks and ships are constrained to lower sails and unstep their mast to enter the port. The king of this mainland is called Mon. He has twenty kings under him and is subject to the King of China, and his city is called Baranaci. And it is there that is Cathay the Great of the east.‡ Hau§ is a cold and high island, where there are copper, silver, pearls and silk, and its king is named Raia Zzotru Mli. The King of Iaulla is called Raia Chetissirimiga; and the King of Guio, Raia Sudacali. And all these three places are cold and on the mainland. Triagomba and Trianpha are two islands to [from] which come pearls, copper, silver and silk, and their king is named Raia Rrom. Bassibassa is [on the] mainland. Then there are Sumdit and Pradit, two islands very

---

* Chincheo, in Fukien.

† The name is that given in the 16th century to the Lequios or Ryukyu Islands, but Pigafetta locates it on the mainland.

‡ This is confused. Cathay, properly northern China, had in the late Middle Ages come to signify the whole country. Mon is perhaps an echo of Mangi, the southern part of China, south of the Yellow River.

§ Probably Hainan.

rich in gold, where the men wear a large jewel of very rich gold on their foot and round their leg. In certain mountains near there, on the mainland, are peoples who kill their fathers and mothers when they are old, that they suffer no more pain. And all the peoples of those places are heathen.

On Tuesday night drawing toward Wednesday the eleventh day of February, one thousand five hundred and twenty-two, having departed from the island of Timor, we entered the great sea named Laut Chidol,★ and laying course between west and southwest we left on the right hand to the north (for fear of the King of Portugal) the island of Zamatra (named by the ancients Traprobana).† Then there are the islands of Pegu, Bengala, Vrizza, Chelin where dwell the Malabari under the King of Marsingue, Calicut under the same king, and Cambaia where dwell the Gurazati, Cananor, Gon, Armux‡ and all the other coasts of India the Great.

In this India the Great are six sorts of men: Nairi, Pamenali, Irauai, Panggelini, Macuai and Poleai.§ Of these, the Nairi are the chiefs, the Panichali are the townsmen; and these two kinds of men consort together. The Irauai gather the palm wine and figs. The Panggelini are the seamen. The Macuai are the fishermen. The Poleai sow and harvest the rice. These last dwell always in the fields and never enter any city, and when they are given something they lay it on the ground and then take it. When these men go through the streets they cry *Po, po, po*, that is to say, Beware of me. It happened (as we were told) that a Nair was by mischance struck by a Poleai, where-upon the Nair, not wishing to abide in this disgrace, caused the Poleai to be killed.

In order to round the Cape of Good Hope we went as far south as

★ Javanese words meaning 'South Sea', *i.e.* the Indian Ocean which they were now entering.

† Taprobana, the classical name for Ceylon, was generally equated with Sumatra in 16th-century cartography.

‡ Identifications: Pegu, Bengal, Orissa, Quilon in Malabar, Calicut, Cambay and Gujarat, Cananor, Goa, Ormuz.

§ Pigafetta's account of the Hindu castes is confused. There are only four main castes: priests, warriors, husbandmen, and the servile caste.

forty-two degrees toward the Antarctic Pole. We remained near this Cape for seven weeks with sails furled because of the west and northwest wind on our bow, and in a very great storm.* This Cape is in the latitude of thirty-four and a half degrees, and one thousand and sixty leagues from the Cape of Malacca. And it is the greatest and most perilous cape in the world. Some of our men, both sick and healthy, wished to go to a place of the Portuguese called Mozambique, because the ship was taking in much water, and also for the great cold, and still more because we had nothing else to eat except rice and water, since for want of salt the meat which we had was rotten and putrefied. But some others, more mindful of their honour than of their own life, determined to go to Spain alive or dead.

At the length, by God's help, on the sixth of May we passed this Cape at a distance of five leagues from it, and had we not approached so close to it we should never have been able to pass it. Then we sailed northwest for two months continually without taking any refreshment or repose. And in that short space of time twenty-one of our men died. And when we cast the Christians into the sea they sank with face upward toward heaven, and the Indians always with face downward. And if God had not given us good weather, we should all have died of hunger. At length, constrained by our great need, we went to the islands of Cape Verde.

On Wednesday the ninth of July we arrived at one of these islands, named Santiago, where we immediately sent the boat ashore to obtain provisions, under pretext and colour of telling the Portuguese that our foremast had broken under the equinoctial line (although it had been at the Cape of Good Hope) and that, while we were refitting our ships, our captain-general with the other two ships had gone before to Spain. So with our merchandise and these good words we obtained two boatloads of rice. And we charged our men in the boat that, when they were ashore, they should ask what day it was. They were answered that to the Portuguese it was Thursday, at which they were much amazed, for to us it was

* In the storm on 16 May, the ship lost her fore-topmast and sprung the fore-yard; and the Cape was not in fact rounded until 19 May.

Wednesday, and we knew not how we had fallen into error. For every day I, being always in health, had written down each day without any intermission. But, as we were told since, there had been no mistake, for we had always made our voyage westward and had returned to the same place of departure as the sun, wherefore the long voyage had brought the gain of twenty-four hours, as is clearly seen.

The boat having gone ashore once more to obtain rice, thirteen of our men with the boat were detained, because one of them (as we learned later in Spain) told the Portuguese that our captain was dead and many others, and that we dared not go to Spain, fearing still to be taken by some caravels. Wherefore we immediately departed thence.*

On Saturday the sixth of September, one thousand five hundred and twenty-two, we entered the Bay of San Lúcar, and we were only eighteen men, the most part sick, of the sixty remaining who had left Molucca, some of whom died of hunger, others deserted at the island of Timor, and others had been put to death for their crimes. From the time when we departed from that Bay until the present day we had sailed fourteen thousand four hundred and sixty leagues, and completed the circuit of the world from east to west.

On Monday the eighth of September we cast anchor near the Mole of Seville, and there we discharged all the artillery. And on Tuesday we all went, in our shirts and barefoot, and each with a torch in his hand, to visit the shrine of Santa Maria de la Victoria and that of Santa Maria de Antigua.

Departing from Seville, I went to Valladolid, where I presented to his Sacred Majesty Don Carlos,† not gold or silver, but something to be prized by such a lord. And among other things I gave him a book written by my hand treating of all the things that had occurred day by day on our voyage. Then I departed thence, and went to Portugal, where I spoke with the King, Dom João,‡ of the things which I

---

* The thirteen men left at Santiago were soon after repatriated in a Portuguese ship from India.

† The Emperor Charles V.   ‡ King John III of Portugal.

had seen. And, passing through Spain, I came into France where I made a gift of some things from the other hemisphere to Madame the Regent, mother of the very Christian King Francois.★ Then I came into Italy, where I established my abode forever, and I devoted my vacations and vigils to the most illustrious and noble lord, Philippe de Villiers l'Isle-Adam, the very worthy Grand Master of Rhodes.

END

★ Louise of Savoy, mother of King Francis I of France.

Set in 12 point Van Dijck type leaded 1 point

with Old English Text for display.

Text printed by W & J Mackay Limited, Chatham

on Mellotex cartridge paper.

Illustrations printed lithography by

Alabaster Passmore & Sons Limited, Maidstone.

Bound by W & J Mackay Limited

in Chiltern cloth blocked with a special design

by Elizabeth Trimby.

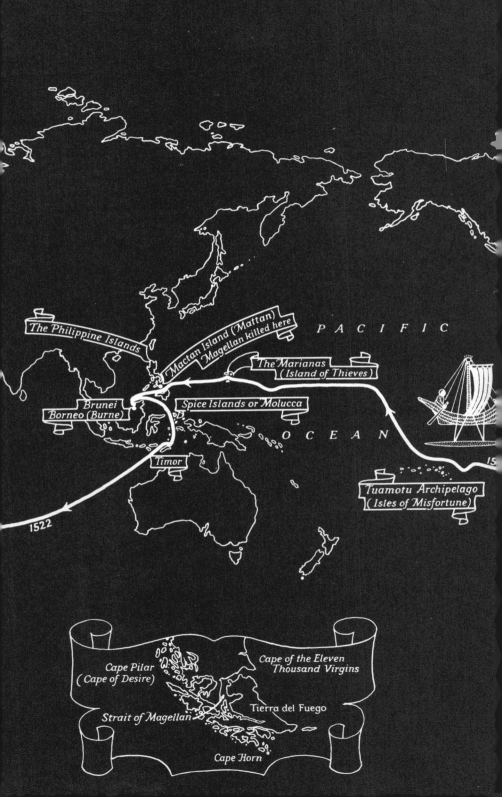

The Philippine Islands

Mactan Island (Mattan)
Magellan killed here

PACIFIC

The Marianas
(Island of Thieves

Brunei
Borneo (Burne)

Spice Islands or Molucca

OCEAN

Timor

Tuamotu Archipelago
(Isles of Misfortune)

15

1522

Cape of the Eleven
Thousand Virgins

Cape Pilar
(Cape of Desire)

Tierra del Fuego

Strait of Magellan

Cape Horn